Powell Lectures on Philosophy
at Indiana University
W. Harry Jellema, Editor

—

FIFTH SERIES

—

GOD AND PHILOSOPHY

GOD AND

PHILOSOPHY

BY

ÉTIENNE GILSON

Published for Indiana University.

NEW HAVEN

YALE UNIVERSITY PRESS

London, Geoffrey Cumberlege, Oxford University Press.

THE
MAHLON POWELL FOUNDATION

Mahlon Powell—1842–1928
Wabash, Indiana

Extract from the last Will and Testament of Mahlon Powell:

Having entertained a desire for many years to assist in the cause of a higher education for the young men and women of our state and nation, and to that end provide a fund to be held in trust for the same, and to select a proper school or university where the same would continue in perpetuity, I will, devise and bequeath all of the real and personal property that I possess and of which I die seized to the Trustees of Indiana University, Bloomington, Indiana, to be held by them and their successors in office forever, the *Income* only to be used and applied in the support and maintenance of a *Chair* in *Philosophy* in said institution, and to be dedicated and forever known as "The Mahlon Powell Professorship in Philosophy" of said University.

In accordance with the provisions of this bequest, the Trustees of Indiana University have established a Chair in Philosophy on The Mahlon Powell Foundation. Each year a Visiting Professor will be invited to fill this Chair. The fifth lecturer on The Mahlon Powell Foundation is Étienne Gilson of the Pontifical Institute of Mediaeval Studies, Toronto.

Herman B Wells
President, Indiana University

CONTENTS

PREFACE

THESE four lectures deal with but one aspect of the highest of all metaphysical problems, and they deal with it on the basis of but a very limited number of historical facts, themselves rather taken for granted than technically established. The problem is the metaphysical problem of God. The particular aspect of this problem singled out for detailed examination is the relation which obtains between our notion of God and the demonstration of his existence. The approach to this philosophical question is the same as I have already presented in *The Unity of Philosophical Experience* (Scribner, New York, 1937) and in *Reason and Revelation in the Middle Ages* (Scribner, New York, 1938). It consists of extracting from the history of past philosophies the essential data that enter into the correct formulation of a philosophical problem, and of determining, in the light of such data, its correct solution.

This is by no means the only conceivable approach to philosophical truth. Neither is it a new one. Its incomparable models are to be found in several dialogues of Plato, for instance, in the *Theaetetus*, the *Philebus*, and the *Parmenides*. Aristotle has explicitly resorted to it, and successfully exploited it, in Book I of his *Metaphysics*. Naturally enough, it is attended by dangers of its own that arise from its very nature. First of all, it can deteriorate into a mere dialectical game wherein philosophical dogmas are debased into philosophical opinions, each of which is successively shown as true from its own point of view and as false from the viewpoint of any other one. The form of corruption proper to the philosophical method of the Academy is best exemplified by the Neo-Academy. But the same approach can also deteriorate into a history of the various philosophies taken as so many concrete, individual, and consequently irreducible facts. Now, while it is true that the history of philosophies is in itself a perfectly legitimate, and even a necessary, branch of historical learning, its very essence as history forbids it to aim at other than historical conclusions. Plato, Aristotle, Descartes, Kant have thought this and that on such and such philosophical questions. After ascertaining such facts, and making them intelligible by all the means at its disposal, the history of philosophies has exhausted its own program. But where it ends, philosophy can begin its own task, which is to judge the answers given to philosophical problems by Plato, Aristotle, Descartes, and Kant in the light of the necessary data of these problems themselves. The historical approach to philosophy uses the history of philosophies as a handmaid to philosophy.

Like everything else, this can be well done or

badly done. Of all the bad ways to do it, the
worst is probably that of some textbooks of
dogmatic philosophy, in which a certain doctrine, posited as true, is used as a criterion to
determine automatically the truth or falsity of
all others. There is but one order of knowledge
where such a method legitimately applies, and
that is revealed theology. If we believe by faith
that God has spoken, since what God says is
true, all that contradicts the word of God can,
and must, be at once excluded as false. The familiar formula of Saint Thomas Aquinas, *Per
hoc autem excluditur error*, is a perfect expression of such a theological attitude. But this
formula cannot be transferred from theology to
philosophy unless it first receive some qualification. The word of God excludes all contrary errors because, *qua* word of God, the word of God
is true. The word of no philosopher, on the contrary, can exclude contrary statements as false,
because the word of no philosopher is true *qua*
the word of this philosopher. If what he says is
true, what excludes all contrary errors is that
which makes what he says true, namely, his suc-
cess both in correctly posing a certain problem
and in doing justice to all the data required for
its solution. If, in the following pages, Thomas
Aquinas appears a bit too much like the *deus ex
machina* of some abstract metaphysical drama,
the ready objection will be that I have spoken as
a Thomist, measuring all the other philosophies

by the yardstick of Thomism. I beg at least to
assure my readers that if I have done this—
which is but too possible—I have committed
what appears to me personally as the one un-
forgivable sin against the very essence of philosophy. Yet, before condemning me for such a
crime, they will have to make sure that I have
actually committed it.

I was educated in a French Catholic college,
which I left, after seven years of studies, without having heard even once, at least as far as I
remember, the name of Saint Thomas Aquinas.
When the time came for me to study philosophy
I went to a state-controlled college, whose professor of philosophy, a belated disciple of Victor Cousin, had certainly never read a line of
Thomas Aquinas. At the Sorbonne, no one of
my professors knew anything about his doctrine.
All that I learned concerning it was that, were
anyone enough of a fool to read it, he would find
there an expression of that Scholasticism which,
since the time of Descartes, had become a mere
piece of mental archeology. To me, however,
philosophy was neither Descartes nor even
Kant; it was Bergson, the genius whose lectures
still remain in my memory as so many hours of
intellectual transfiguration. Henri Bergson is
the only living master in philosophy I have ever
had, and I consider it as one of the greatest
blessings bestowed by God on my philosophical
life that, owing to Bergson, I have met philo-

sophical genius both somewhere else and otherwise than in books. Yet, even though Bergson
says that, ever since his earliest philosophical
efforts, he has always been on his way toward
the God of the Jewish-Christian tradition, he
himself did not at that time know it; at any
rate, nobody has ever been led by Bergson to the
philosophical method of Saint Thomas Aquinas.

The man to whom I am indebted for my first
knowledge of Saint Thomas was a Jew. He had
never opened a single one of the works of
Thomas, nor did he intend ever to do so. But he
was, besides many other good things, a man of
an almost uncanny intelligence, with a surprising gift of seeing facts in an impartial, cold, and
objective light, just as they were. As soon as I
had attended the course of lectures in Hume he
was then giving at the Sorbonne, I realized that,
to me, to understand any philosophy would always mean to approach it as I had seen Lucien
Lévy-Bruhl approach that of Hume. When, two
years later, I went to him for a subject of a
thesis, he advised me to study the vocabulary
and, eventually, the matter borrowed from Scholasticism by Descartes. Hence the book which I
have since published under the title: *La Liberté
chez Descartes et la théologie.* Historically
speaking, this work is now out of date, but its
nine long years of preparation taught me two
things: first, to read Saint Thomas Aquinas;
secondly, that Descartes had vainly tried to

solve, by means of his own famous method, philosophical problems whose only correct position and solution were inseparable from the method of Saint Thomas Aquinas. In other words (and my surprise can still be found naïvely expressed in the last pages of that now old book), I discovered that the only context in which the metaphysical conclusions of Descartes made sense was the metaphysics of Saint Thomas Aquinas.

To say that this came to me as a shock would be unduly to dramatize what was but the objective conclusion of patient historical observations. Since, however, it had become clear to me that, technically speaking, the metaphysics of Descartes had largely been a clumsy overhauling of scholastic metaphysics, I decided to learn metaphysics from those who had really known it, namely, those very Schoolmen whom my own professors of philosophy felt the more free to despise as they had never read them. Their study has wholly convinced me, not at all that to philosophize consists in repeating what they have said, but rather that no philosophical progress will ever be possible unless we first learn to know what they knew. The chaotic condition of contemporary philosophy, with the ensuing moral, social, political, and pedagogical chaos, is not due to any lack of philosophical insight among modern thinkers; it simply follows from the fact that we have lost our way because we have lost

the knowledge of some fundamental principles
which, since they are true, are the only ones on
which, today as well as in Plato's own day, any
philosophical knowledge worthy of the name can
possibly be established. If anybody be afraid of
sterilizing his own precious philosophical per-
sonality by simply learning how to think, let
him read the books of Jacques Maritain as a
sedative for his fears of intellectual barrenness.
The great curse of modern philosophy is the almost universally prevailing rebellion against intellectual self-discipline. Where loose thinking
obtains, truth cannot possibly be grasped,
whence the conclusion naturally follows that
there is no truth.

The following lectures rest on the contrary
assumption that truth can be found, even in
metaphysics. They do not contain anything like
a history of the philosophical problem of God;
important doctrines have been barely sketched,
while innumerable others have not been mentioned at all. Neither do they pretend to be a
sufficient demonstration of the existence of God.
Their aim and scope are rather to achieve the
clear and precise determination of a certain
metaphysical problem. I would like to think
that, after reading them, some among my readers will at least understand the meaning of their
own words, when they say that the existence of
God cannot be demonstrated. Nobody really
knows that this cannot be done unless he realizes

at least what it would be to do it. The only philosopher who has made me clearly realize the full metaphysical implications of this problem is Saint Thomas Aquinas. I am as fond of my own intellectual freedom as anyone else, but I want to be free to agree with somebody when I think that what he says is right. Saint Thomas Aquinas never thought of anything like a "Thomistic truth." These words do not even make sense. Judging various answers to the problem of God on the ground of their relative aptness to do justice to all its demands, I have come to the conclusion that the best answer to it has been given by the man who, because he was the first to grasp the deepest implications of this problem, has also been the first freely to bow to the metaphysical necessity of its only solution. Anybody who can is still today welcome to do the same thing as freely as Thomas Aquinas himself ever did it. As to him who either cannot or will not do it, let him have at least the satisfaction of turning down the only pertinent solution to a true problem: not the supreme carpenter of Paley or the supreme watchmaker of Voltaire, but the infinite act of self-existence, by whom all the rest is, and as compared with whom all the rest is as though it were not.

I would like to express my gratitude to the Board of Trustees of Indiana University which approved my appointment as Visiting Professor of Philosophy on the Mahlon Powell Foundation, for 1939–40. I will perhaps be permitted to say how particularly grateful I feel to the members of the department of Philosophy of Indiana University for so graciously welcoming me at a time when men of different nations feel little inclination unreservedly to trust one another. But I must quite especially thank Professor W. Harry Jellema. His letter of invitation so clearly outlined and defined for me the task I was desired to undertake, that to quote one of its sentences remains perhaps my best chance, if not to justify the contents of these lectures, at least to make clear their general intention: "For too many philosophers today, philosophy no longer means anything of what it ought to mean; and for almost all our contemporaries Christianity has nothing to say which science has not disproved, nor anything intellectually respectable which had not already been said by the Greeks." It has been my intention to show, on the particular problem of God, that the Christian philosophers have said, owing to the Greeks, things that had never been said by the Greeks themselves; that these things are so intellectually respectable that they have become part and parcel of modern philosophy; and that, though no one can expect science to prove them, we should not mistakenly accept as their disproval by science the failure of some scientists to understand the fundamental problems of metaphysics.

These lectures are printed exactly as they were read at Indiana University and as they were written at the Pontifical Institute of Mediaeval Studies, Toronto. It is an uncommon blessing to live in such a place, where friends patiently suffer one to try on them his provisorily last ideas about any and every question. To the name of the Rev. G. B. Phelan, President of the Pontifical Institute of Mediaeval Studies, who never failed to help me through my philosophical adventures, I must this time add the name of my eminent friend Professor Jacques Maritain. To both of them I feel deeply indebted for confirmations, suggestions, and corrections, which, I am sure, have made this little book a little less unworthy of its subject.

ÉTIENNE GILSON

Pontifical Institute of Mediaeval Studies

GOD AND PHILOSOPHY

I

GOD AND GREEK PHILOSOPHY

IN the history of Western Culture, every chapter begins with the Greeks. This is true of logic, of science, of art, of politics, and it is equally true of natural theology; but it is not at once clear where one should look, in the past of ancient Greece, for the origins of our philosophical notion of God.

As soon as we read the texts of Aristotle whence most of our information concerning early Greek philosophy is derived, the difficulty appears in full. Speaking of Thales the Milesian, Aristotle says that, according to this philosopher, the first principle, or element, or substance, of which all things are born and to which all things ultimately return, is water. To which Aristotle adds, in another text, that according to the same Thales "all things are full of gods."[1] How can these two distinct statements be philosophically reconciled?

A first way to do it is to identify the two notions of water and of divinity. This is what a modern scholar has done by making Thales

1. Aristotle, *Metaphysics*, I, 3, 983b, 20–27; *De Anima*, I, 5, 411a, 8.

say that water is not only a god but the supreme god. In such an interpretation of the texts, "the supreme god, and the cosmogenetic god, are one divine power, Water."[2] The only difficulty in accepting this simple and logical solution of the problem is that it ascribes to Thales several ideas which he may very well have held, but of which Aristotle says absolutely nothing.[3] According to the earliest testimonies at our disposal, Thales did not say that water was a god, or that, among the gods which crowd this world, there was a supreme god; consequently he has not said that water

2. R. Kenneth Hack, *God in Greek Philosophy to the Time of Socrates* (Princeton University Press, 1931), p. 42.

3. Aristotle has nowhere reconstructed the thought of Thales along the lines followed by modern scholars. In his *De Anima,* I, 5, 411a, 7, he relates as another opinion of Thales that the magnet has a soul, since it is able to move iron; whence Aristotle himself infers, obviously as a conjecture, that Thales' statement "all things are full of gods" had perhaps been inspired by the opinion that "soul is diffused throughout the whole universe." For an English translation of the texts related to Thales, see Milton C. Nahm, *Selections from Early Greek Philosophy* (F. S. Crofts, New York, 1930), pp. 59–62. After Aristotle, and chiefly under Stoic influences, the doctrine of the world-soul was ascribed to Thales, until Cicero (*De Nat. Deorum,* I, 25) completed the circle by identifying the so-called world-soul of Thales with God. Cf. John Burnet, *Early Greek Philosophy* (4th ed. London, A. and C. Black, 1930), pp. 49–50. All this is a later reconstruction of the doctrine of Thales, and there is no authentic historical evidence to support it.

was the supreme god. Here, in a nutshell, is
what is to remain for us the whole problem.
On the one side, a man posits a certain natural
element as the very stuff this world is made of.
Let us call it water, but the name does not make
any difference, and the problem will remain
identically the same when the first principle is
called fire, air, the Indeterminate, or even the
Good. On the other side, the same man posits
as a sort of axiom that all things are full of
gods. Whence our own immediate conclusion
that, to him, water is not only one of the gods,
but the greatest of all. Yet the more logical
such an inference appears to us, the more surprising it should seem that this man himself
did not think of drawing it. There is at least
an off chance that, were he now confronted by
us with our own inference, he might object to
it as to an illegitimate one. In short, instead of
writing the history of philosophy as it has
been, we write the history of what philosophy
should have been. A very bad way to write the
history of philosophy indeed, and, as will soon
be seen, a sure way to miss its deepest philosophical meaning.

Another method to get rid of our difficulty
is, instead of turning water into a god, to turn
the god of Thales into water. This was exactly
the purpose John Burnet had in mind when

he advised his readers not "to make too much
of the saying that all things are full of gods."[4]
What lies behind Burnet's advice is his absolute conviction that "there is no trace of theological speculation" either in Thales the Milesian or in his immediate successors. In other
words, when Thales says that the world is full
of gods, he does not really means "gods." He
simply means some physical and purely natural energy, such as water, for instance, which,
according to his own doctrine, is the first
principle of all things. The same observation
should apply to the successors of Thales.
When Anaximander says that his own first
principle, the Indeterminate, is divine, or
when Anaximenes teaches that infinite air is
the first cause of all that is, including gods
and divine beings, they do not think of the
gods as possible objects of worship. In Burnet's own words, "this non-religious use of the
word *god* is characteristic of the whole period"
of early Greek philosophy,[5] to which my only
objection is that very few words have a more
distinctly religious connotation than the word
"god." Everybody is welcome to interpret the

4. J. Burnet, *op. cit.*, p. 50.
5. *Ibid.*, pp. 13, 14, and 50. Burnet's rationalistic interpretation of early Greek philosophy is itself a reaction
against the sociological interpretation of it developed in
F. C. Cornford, *From Religion to Philosophy* (London,

sentence, "All things are full of gods," as meaning that there is not a single god in anything,
but the least that can be said of it is that it is
a rather bold interpretation.

Instead of making Thales say either that
his gods are but water or that his water is a
god, why not try this third historical hypothesis, namely, that as a rule philosophers mean
to say just what they do say? It is a risky
business to teach Greek to a Greek. Were we
asked what were the exact connotations of the
word "god" in a Greek mind of the fifth century B.C., I would at once admit that this is
a very difficult question to answer. Yet we
might try, and the best way for us to do it
would probably be to read first the works in
which the origin, the nature, and the functions of what the Greeks called the "gods"
have been described at some length. There is
Homer, for instance, and there is Hesiod. And
I know full well that, even concerning Homer
himself, it has been maintained that where he
says "god" he does not mean "god." But
surely there is no harm in our asking him what
he does mean; and before turning down his

1912). Burnet does not want us "to fall into the error of
deriving science from mythology" (*op. cit.*, p. 14). In
which, as I think, Burnet is right, but if it is a mistake to
derive Thales' science from mythology, it is another mistake to eliminate mythology from Thales' science.

answer, we should at least give it all due consideration.[6]

The first striking fact about the Greek meaning of this word is that its origin is not a philosophical one. When the early Greek philosophers began to speculate, the gods were already there, and the philosophers merely inherited them from those men whom all antiquity, up to the time of Saint Augustine, has called the Theologian Poets. To limit ourselves to Homer's *Iliad*, the word "god" there seems to apply to an incredible variety of different objects. A Greek god could be conceived as what we ourselves would call a person, as happened in the case of Zeus, Hera, Apollo, Pallas Athena, in short, of all the so-called Olympians. But the god could just as well be some physical reality, such as, for instance, the great god Ocean, or the Earth itself, or the Sky. When, at the beginning of the *Iliad*, XX, Zeus bade Themis call the gods to council, "there was no River came not up,

6. On the position of Wilamowitz, Rohde, and Edward Meyer, see the judicious remarks of R. K. Hack, *op. cit.*, pp. 4–6. Homer has been considered by some of his modern interpreters as being not only irreligious, but even antireligious. According to some others, on the contrary, he was a religious reformer and, so to speak, the Saint Paul of early Greek paganism. Such is, for instance, the position of Gilbert Murray, *Five Stages of Greek Religion* (New York, Columbia University Press, 1925), p. 82.

save only Ocean, nor any Nymph, of all that
haunt fair thickets and springs of rivers and
grassy water meadows."[7] Nor is this all. Even
the great natural fatalities which govern all
mortal lives appear to us in Homer's *Iliad* as
so many gods. Such are Terror, Rout, and
Strife; and such also are Death, and Sleep,
the lord of gods and men, who is the brother
of Death.

At first sight, it does not seem easy to find
common elements in this heterogeneous med-
ley of beings, of things, and even of mere abstractions. On closer inspection, however, there
appears at least one. Whatever the real nature
of what they designate, these names of gods
all point to living powers, or forces, endowed
with a will of their own, operating in human

7. *Homeri Ilias,* ed. Thomas W. Allen (Oxford, Claren-
don Press, 1931), 3 vols. The verse will be quoted from
this edition; but the texts will be quoted from *The Iliad
of Homer,* trans. by A. Lang, W. Leaf, and Ernest Myers
(New York), The Modern Library. Cf. Bk. XX, vv. 7–9,
p. 368. It is noteworthy that even the personal Greek gods
seem to have originally been but personalized natural
forces—Zeus, G. Murray says, "is the Achaean sky-god,"
Phoebus Apollo "is a sun-god," Pallas Athena is "the
Dawn-goddess, Eos," associated with Athens (*op. cit.,*
pp. 71–74). On the psychological problems raised by this
personalizing process, see the always suggestive and penetrating remarks of R. K. Hack, *op. cit.,* pp. 12–16. On
Greek religious life and feelings, see A. J. Festugière,
L'Idéal religieux des Grecs et l'Évangile (Paris, Gabalda,
1932), pp. 20–32.

lives and swaying human destinies from above.
The popular pinkish picture of Ancient
Greece as the seat of an intelligent race leading a carefree life in the peaceful enjoyment
of a friendly nature and under the guidance of
good-natured gods does not agree too well
with what we learn from the Greek epics, from
the Greek tragedies, or even from the political
history of Greece. At any rate it is wholly at
variance with what is known of Greek religion.
A religious-minded Greek felt himself an in-
strument in the hands of innumerable divine
powers to which not only his acts but even his
thoughts were ultimately submitted. As everybody knows, from its very first verses the subject of Homer's *Iliad* is the wrath of Achilles
and the disasters it brought on the Greeks.
Now the cause for the wrath of Achilles was
his unjust treatment by King Agamemnon.
As to the cause of this unjust treatment, Agamemnon himself tells us what it was: "It is not
I who am the cause, but Zeus, and Erynis that
walketh in the darkness, who put into my soul
fierce madness on the day when in the as-
sembly I, even I, bereft Achilles of his meed.
What could I do? It is god who accomplisheth
all."[8]

8. Cf. Homer, *Iliad,* Bk. XIX, vv. 86–90, English trans.,
p. 357. This point is later on confirmed by Achilles him-

The first characteristic of these divine powers is life. Whatever else he may happen to be,
a Greek god never is an inanimate thing; he is
a living being, just as men themselves are,
with the sole difference that whereas human
life is bound sometime to come to an end, the
Greek gods never die. Hence their other name:
the Immortals.[9] And the second characteristic
of these Immortals is that all of them are related much more to man than to the world at
large. Let us take, almost at random, any one
of those permanent fatalities that sway the
lives of men; it is a god. Such are Earth, Sky,
Ocean; all the Rivers which bring life to man
by fecundating his fields or threaten him with
death by overflowing their banks; such also
are Sleep and Death, Fear and Strife, im-
placable Vengeance, and Rout, and Rumor
who is the Messenger of Zeus. But we should

self: "Father Zeus, sore madness dealest thou verily to
men. Never could the son of Atreus (i.e. Agamemnon)
have stirred the soul within my breast, nor led off the
damsel (i.e. Briseis) implacably against my will, had not
Zeus willed that on many of the Achaians death should
come" (Bk. XIX, vv. 270–274, English trans., p. 362).
Every Greek poem, like every Greek tragedy, presupposes
a "Prelude in Heaven" which gives the poem, or the
tragedy, its full meaning.

9. The two notions of life and of blood are inseparable
in a Greek mind. Since the Greek gods have no blood,
they cannot lose it, and consequently they cannot die.
Cf. *Iliad*. Bk. V, vv. 339–342, English trans., p. 84.

not forget, after the dreadful divinities, the benevolent ones: Justice, Love, and the Muses, and the Graces; in short, all the immortally living powers which rule the lives of mortal men.

To these two characteristics let us add still a third one. A divine power that reigns supreme in its own order may have to yield, on some definite points, to other gods equally supreme in their own order. For instance, although the Immortals never die, they sleep; Sleep then is "the lord of all gods and of all men."[10] This is a universal law. Just as they sleep, the Immortals love and desire; hence the words of the goddess Hera to Aphrodite: "Give me now Love and Desire wherewith thou overcomest all the Immortals, and mortal men." Hera, the only divinity whom Zeus is really afraid of, whom he seldom sees without feeling "sore troubled" because "she upbraideth him ever amid the immortal gods"; in short, the most powerful divinity by whom any man's life can be swayed, his wife.

Yet, the only absolute power to which Zeus himself is submitted does not rule him from without but from within. It is his own will. The greatest of all gods, the father of gods

10. *Ibid.*, Bk. XIV, v. 233, English trans., pp. 256–257.

and men, the god of counsel, Zeus himself remains powerless before his own consent, once
given.[11] And Zeus cannot but consent to his
own will, though his will is by no means iden-
tical with his own individual preference. What
is the deeper will of the deeper Zeus is that
everything may happen according to Fate
and to Destiny. When his most beloved son
Sarpedon is engaged in fight against Patroklos, Zeus knows it is fated that Sarpedon
should die. Torn between his fatherly love and
his consent to Fate, Zeus at first hesitates; but
Hera sternly reminds him of his duty: "A
mortal man long doomed to fate dost thou desire to deliver again from death of evil name?
Work thy will, but all we other gods will in no
way praise thee." Thus spoke Hera, "nor did
the father of gods and men disregard her. But
he shed bloody raindrops on the earth, honour-
ing his dear son, that Patroklos was about to
slay."[12] Because the deeper will of Zeus is one
with the invincible power of Fate, Zeus is the
most powerful of all the gods.

If this be true, the definition of a Greek
god should run thus: a god, to any living

11. *Ibid.*, Bk. I, vv. 524–527, English trans., p. 16: "No
word of mine is revocable nor false nor unfulfilled when
the bowing of my head hath pledged it."

12. *Ibid.*, Bk. XVI, vv. 439–461, English trans., p. 302.

being, is any other living being whom he knows
as lording it over his own life. That what happens to a being endowed with life can be explained but by another being also endowed
with life, was to the Greeks a point beyond discussion, and the fact that they felt sure of it
should be to us a strong reminder not to speak
lightly of Greek religion, or of the Greek
gods. A religious-minded Greek felt himself
the passive battlefield of overpowering and
too often mutually conflicting divine influences. His will was at their mercy. As Pindar
says: "From the gods come all the means of
mortal exploits; thanks to the gods are men
wise and brave and eloquent."[13] But the reverse is equally true. The same heroes whom
we see bravely fighting so long as the gods are
with them shamelessly take to their heels as
soon as the same gods desert them. They then
feel what they call "the turning of the sacred
scales of Zeus"; as to Zeus himself, he knows
this turning of the scales because he sees it
happening within his own hands: "When the
fourth time Hector and Achilles had reached
the springs, then the Father hung his golden
balances, and set therein two lots of dreary
death, one of Achilles, one of horse-taming

13. Pindar, *Pythian Odes*, I, vv. 41–42, ed. J. Sandys
(London, 1915), p. 159. Loeb Classical Library.

Hector, and held them by the midst, and poised. Then Hector's fated day sank down, and fell to the house of Hades, and Phoebus Apollo left him."[14] Once more the will of Zeus is reduced to his consent to Destiny; consequently, Hector must die. A world where everything came to men from without, including their feelings and passions, their virtues and their vices, such was the Greek religious world. The immortal beings from whose favor, and disfavor, everything thus came to men—such were the gods of the Greeks.

We are now beginning to realize why it was not so easy for a Greek philosopher to deify his first universal principle of all things. The question is not to know if Thales, Anaximenes, and their successors still believed in the gods of Homer, or if, rather, they had not already begun to eliminate most of them as being mere fabulous imaginings. Granting that this second hypothesis is more likely to be true than the first one, the difficulty remains the same so long as the notion of god still retains something of its religious connotations. If, speaking as a philosopher, you say that everything is x, and that x is a god, you are thereby saying that everything is not only a god but the same god. How then could you add that the

14. *Iliad*, Bk. XXII, vv. 208–213, English trans., p. 406.

world is full of *gods?* If, speaking as a religious man, you begin by positing that the
world is full of gods, either your gods are not
the principles of those things in which they
are, or else, if each god is such a principle, it
can no longer be said that there is but one
principle of all things. Since Thales and his
successors were speaking as philosophers,
their only logical choice was the first one.
They should have said that everything was
but one and the same god, thus reaching at
once the very same materialistic pantheism of
the Stoics wherewith Greek philosophy was
ultimately to end. Abstractly speaking, the
early Greek philosophers could have immediately brought the evolution of Greek natural theology to its close; but they did not, because they did not want to lose their gods.[15]

15. The continuity of the religious and philosophical
Greek thought about God is, on the contrary, strongly
emphasized by R. K. Hack, *op. cit.,* p. 39. We are thus
confronted with two antinomic interpretations of the
same texts. According to Burnet, when Thales says that
"all things are full of gods," he does not really mean
"gods." According to R. K. Hack, the authentic thought
of Thales is that "water is the living and divine substance of the universe" (*ibid.*). In point of fact, in the
text of Aristotle which is the main source of our knowledge of Thales, mention is made of the similar doctrine
of "the first students of the gods" concerning Ocean and
Thetys considered as "parents of generation"; after
which Aristotle adds: "Whether there is such ancient and
early opinion concerning nature would be an obscure

Our first reaction is naturally to blame such a lack of philosophical courage; but there may be less courage in following abstract logic than in refusing to let it play havoc with the manifold of reality. When a philosopher asks himself "What stuff is the world made of?" he is asking a purely objective and impersonal question. When, on the contrary, Agamemnon declares: "What could I do? It is god who accomplisheth all," he is answering this most subjective and personal problem: What has made me act as I did? Now it is not at once evident that correctly to

question; but Thales is said to have expressed this opinion in regard to the first cause." *Metaphysics,* I, 3, 983b, 18–984a, 2; M. C. Nahm, *op. cit.,* pp. 60–61. It is therefore clear that Aristotle had no certitude concerning the continuity of the two doctrines. To blame him for having failed "to include the attribute of divinity along with the Psyche that is diffused through all things" (R. K. Hack, *op. cit.,* p. 42, n.), is also to take it for granted that Aristotle should have done so, which is by no means proved. To conclude, Burnet links together these two statements, "All things are full of gods," "The magnet is alive" (*op. cit.,* p. 48), so as to suggest that, to Thales, the gods are physical forces of the same sort as the magnet; R. K. Hack links together the two statements: "All things are full of gods," and "There is a soul diffused through all things," so as to suggest that the world-soul is God. Aristotle, on the contrary, has never linked together any two of these various theses, and has not even explicitly ascribed the doctrine of the world-soul to Thales (*De Anima,* I, 5, 411a, 7–9). The fact that some scholars eliminate god from texts where god is, does not authorize us to put god in texts where god is not.

answer the first problem is also to solve the
second one. We might well try to quench Agamemnon's curiosity by telling him that, since
everything is water, the reason why he has
bereft Achilles of his meed must have had
something to do with water. I think he would
listen to our explanation, but we may be sure
that by the word "water" he would at once
understand the god Ocean; to which his ready
objection would surely be that our answer is
the wrong answer because our god is the
wrong god. Not Okeanos, King Agamemnon
would say, but Blind Folly (Ate) is the only
conceivable cause for such mad behavior on
my part.[16] Blind Folly is a god; water is but
a thing.

When Greek philosophers themselves used
the word "god," they too had in mind a cause
which was more than a mere thing, whence for
them the difficulty of finding for the problem
of the world order a single and all-compre-
hensive solution. As philosophers, even the
very first Greek thinkers appear to us as perfect representatives of a truly scientific attitude of mind. To them reality was essentially
what they could touch and see, and their fundamental question about it was: What is it?
To the question: What is the Ocean? the an-

16. *Iliad,* Bk. XIX, vv. 91–92, p. 357.

swer, He is a god, simply does not make sense.[17] Conversely, to the question: What is the world? the formula, "All things are full of gods," cannot possibly do for an answer. Taking the world as a given reality, the Greek philosophers simply asked themselves what its "nature" was, that is, what was the essential substance of all things and the hidden principle of all their operations? Was it water, or air, or fire, or the Indeterminate? Or was it perhaps a mind, a thought, an Idea, a law? Whatever answer they might give to their problem, the Greek philosophers always found themselves confronted with nature as with a self-explaining fact. "Nothing can come into being from that which is not," Demokritos says, "nor pass away into that which is not."[18] Had it been possible for nature not to be, it would have never existed. Now nature is there; hence it has always been there, and ever shall be. So necessary and eternal was a

17. This is true of even the theogony of Hesiod (cf. R. K. Hack, *op. cit.*, chap. iii, pp. 23–32). Much more systematic than that of Homer, the hesiodic *Theogony* still essentially remains a theology, that is to say, a religious explanation of the world by means of certain persons, not a philosophical explanation of the world by means of one or several natural things. Mythology is religion, philosophy is knowledge, and although true religion and true knowledge ultimately agree, they represent two distinct types of problems, demonstration and solutions.

18. Text in M. C. Nahm, *op. cit.*, p. 165, n. 44.

nature thus understood, that when a Greek philosopher found himself driven to the conclusion that this world of ours must have had a beginning and is destined some day to reach its end, he would immediately conceive both the beginning and the end of this world as but two moments in an eternal cycle of ever-recurring events. As Simplicius says: "Those who assumed innumerable worlds, for instance Anaximander, Leukippos, Demokritos and, at a later date, Epicurus, held that they came into being and passed away *ad infinitum,* some always coming into being and others passing away."[19] If this cannot be considered as a scientifically proved answer to the problem of nature, it is at least the adequate philosophical expression of what an exhaustive scientific explanation of the world of nature should be. This type of explanation falls short where it takes itself for an answer to the specifically distinct problems of religion.

Whether such scientifically unanswerable problems should be asked or not is a legitimate question, but it is not our present question.

19. Cf. J. Burnet, *op. cit.,* p. 59. Concerning Anaximander, see texts in M. C. Nahm, *op. cit.,* pp. 62, 63; on Leukippos and Demokritos, *op. cit.,* pp. 160–161, or J. Burnet, *op. cit.,* pp. 338–339. The best work on this question is that of A. Dies, *Le Cycle mystique* (Paris, F. Alean, 1909).

We are now dealing with historical facts. Now one of these facts is that the Greeks themselves have constantly raised specifically religious problems; another one is that they have given these problems specifically religious answers; and it is a third fact that the greatest among the Greek philosophers have found it very hard, not to say impossible, to reconcile their religious interpretation of the world with its philosophical interpretation.

The only element common to their two views of nature was a sort of general feeling that, for whatever reason things may be happening, that which is happening could not possibly not happen. Hence the often-propounded view of the history of Greek philosophy, which shows it as a progressive rationalization of primitive Greek religion. Yet there are difficulties. The religious notions of Fate and Destiny are specifically distinct from the philosophical notion of necessity. That all men, including Hector, must ultimately die is a law of nature; as such it belongs in the philosophical order of necessity. That Hector should die at an appointed time and under definite circumstances is an event in a particular human life. Behind necessity, there is a law; behind Fate, there is a will.

The same relation which obtains between

necessity and fate also obtains between the philosophical notion of cause and the Greek notion of the gods. A first cause, or principle, is a universally valid explanation for all that is, has ever been, or ever shall be. As an object of scientific or of philosophical knowledge, man is but one among the countless things that are possible objects of empirical observation and of rational explanation. When he looks at his own life as a scientist or as a philosopher, any man views its successive events, and he foresees his own death, as just so many particular effects of impersonal causes. But it so happens that every man is personally acquainted with a type of cause widely different from the scientific and philosophical ones. Man knows himself. Because he knows himself, man can say "I am." And because he knows other things besides himself, he can say of these things: "They are." A fact of tremendous importance indeed, since it is through human knowledge and, as far as we can see, through it alone that the world can achieve the awareness of its own existence. Hence, for the philosophers and the scientists of all times a first not inconsiderable difficulty: since man as a knowing being is part of the world, how to account for nature without ascribing to its first principle either knowledge or something

which, because it virtually contains it, is actually superior to it?

From this same presence of knowledge in
the world, a second difficulty arises, which is a
still more considerable one. As a knowing being, man is able to distinguish between things,
to become acquainted with their specific natures, and consequently to determine his own
attitude toward things after his own knowledge of what they are. Now to be not determined by things but regulated by one's own
knowledge of things is precisely what we call
to be free. By introducing into the world a
certain possibility of choice, knowledge brings
about a curious sort of being which not only
is, or exists, like all the rest, but which is,
or exists, for itself; and for which alone all
the rest appears as a set of actually existing
things. Such a being—and I beg to remind
you that its existence is an observable fact—
cannot but be conscious of the exceptional
.situation it occupies in the universe. In a sense,
it is but a part of the whole and, as such, completely submitted to the laws of the whole. In
another sense, it is itself a whole, because it is
an original center of spontaneous reactions
and of free decisions. We call such a being
man; we say that, since man directs his acts
according to his knowledge, he has a will. As a

cause, a human will is most unlike any other known sort of cause, for it is the only known one to be confronted by possible choices and to be an original power of self-determination. By far the hardest problem for philosophy and for science is to account for the existence of human wills in the world without ascribing to the first principle either a will or something which, because it virtually contains will, is actually superior to it.

To understand this is also to reach the deeply hidden source of Greek mythology, and therefore of Greek religion. The Greek gods are the crude but telling expression of this absolute conviction that since man is somebody, and not merely something, the ultimate explanation for what happens to him should rest with somebody, and not merely with something. As a stream of water running between muddy banks, Skamandros is but a river, that is, a thing; but as a Trojan river which boldly opposes the will of fleet-foot Achilles, it cannot be but a thing. Then does Skamandros appear in the semblance of a man, or rather of a superman, that is to say, of a god. Mythology is not a first step on the path to true philosophy. In fact, it is no philosophy at all. Mythology is a first step on the path to true religion; it is religious in its own right. Greek philosophy cannot have emerged from Greek mythology by any process of progressive rationalization,[20] because Greek philosophy was a rational attempt to understand the world as a world of things, whereas Greek mythology expressed the firm decision of man not to be left alone, the only person in a world of deaf and dumb things.

If this be true, we should not be surprised to see very great Greek philosophers at a loss how to identify their principles with their gods, or their gods with their principles. They needed them both. When Plato says of something that it truly is, or exists, he always means to say that its nature is both necessary and intelligible. Material and sensible things, for instance, cannot truly be said to be, for the simple reason that, ceaselessly changing

20. The theology of Hesiod is much more systematic than the loose theological elements scattered throughout the whole work of Homer. Hence some historians feel strongly inclined to consider it as marking a transitional stage on the road from primitive Greek mythology to early Greek philosophy. Their main argument is the rational tendency, so apparent in the *Theogony* of Hesiod, to reduce Greek mythology to some sort of systematic unity (see L. Robin, *La Pensée grecque* [Paris, 1923], p. 33, interpreted by R. K. Hack, *op. cit.*, p. 24). The fact itself is correct, but a rationally handled theology still remains a theology; a systematically organized mythology is a more rational theology than a loose one, but it is not an inch nearer to being a philosophy.

as they are, none of them ever remains the
same during two successive instants. As soon
as you know one of them, it vanishes, or else it
alters its appearance, so that your knowledge
either has completely lost its object, or no
longer answers its object. How then could
material things be intelligible? Man can know
only that which is. Truly *to be* means to be
immaterial, immutable, necessary, and intelligible. That is precisely what Plato calls Idea.
The eternal and intelligible Ideas are reality
itself. Not this and that particular man, but
their unchangeable essence. The only thing
that truly is, or exists, in a given individual,
is not that accidental combination of charac-
ters which constitutes him as distinct from
every other individual within the same species;
it is rather his own sharing in the eternal essence of this species. Not Socrates as Socrates,
or Callias as Callias, is truly a real being; in
so far as they really are, Socrates and Callias
are one and the same thing, namely Man-in-
Himself, or the Idea of Man.

Such is Plato's view of reality when he sees
it as an object of philosophical knowledge. Let
us now ask ourselves what can deserve the title
of divine in such a philosophy? If that which
is the more real is also the more divine, the
eternal Ideas should eminently deserve to be

called divine. Now, among the Ideas there is
one which dominates all the others, because
they all share in its intelligibility. It is the
Idea of Good. Just as among the gods in
heaven the sun is the lord of all that shares in
the essence of light, the Idea of Good dominates the intelligible world because all that is,
in so far as it is, is good. Why then should we
hesitate to conclude that in Plato's philosophy
the Idea of Good is god?

I am far from disputing the logical validity
of such a deduction. Plato should have made
it. I even agree that we can hardly refrain
from reading as a definition of his own god
the famous lines of the *Republic* where Plato
says of the Idea of Good that it is "the universal author of all things beautiful and right,
parent of light and of the lord of light in the
visible world, and the immediate source of reason and truth in the intellectual; and that this
is the power upon which he who would act rationally either in public or private life must
have his eye fixed."[21] Assuredly, nothing more
closely resembles the definition of the Christian God than this definition of the Good.[22]

21. Plato, *Republic,* 517; quoted from *The Dialogues of
Plato,* trans. B. Jowett, published with an Introduction
by Prof. Raphael Demos (New York, 1937), I, 776.
22. A. J. Festugière, O.P., *op. cit.,* p. 191; by the same
author, *Contemplation et vie contemplative selon Platon*

Yet, when all is said, the fact remains that
Plato himself has never called the Good a god.
To persuade his historians that since Plato
himself does not say that the Good is a god we
had better not make him say it would be a
practically desperate undertaking. Even non-
Christian interpreters of Plato have read
Christian theology into his philosophy, after
which they found it easy to demonstrate that
Christian theology was but a corrupt edition of
Plato's philosophy. It should be permitted,
however, to suggest that if Plato has never
said that the Idea of Good is a god, the reason
for it might be that he never thought of it as
of a god. And why, after all, should an Idea
be considered as a god? An Idea is no person;
it is not even a soul; at best it is an intelligible
cause, much less a person than a thing.[23]

(Paris, J. Vrin, 1936). Cf. "Le Dieu de Platon," in A.
Dies, *Autour de Platon* (Paris, G. Beauchesne, 1927), II,
523–574; and *La Religion de Platon*, pp. 575–602.

23. According to Festugière, the Idea of Good is "the
most divine of all that which is divine," so that he who
climbs the ladder of beings, from sensible things up to
the highest of all Ideas, ultimately grasps the first Being;
"he sees God" (*L'Idéal religieux des Grecs et l'Évangile*,
p. 44; cf. p. 54). In the texts of *Republic*, 508a–509c,
517b–c, which Festugière quotes in support of his asser-
tion, the sun and the stars are called gods, but not the
Ideas. Even the Idea of Good is not called a god. The
other references given by the same historian are *Republic*, 507b; *Phaedo*, 75d–e; *Parmenides*, 130b and ff.; *Philebus*, 15a. In not one of these texts have I been able to find

What makes it so hard for some modern
scholars to reconcile themselves to this fact is
that after so many centuries of Christian
thought it has become exceedingly difficult for
us to imagine a world where the gods are not
the highest reality, while that which is the
most supremely real in it is not a god. It is a
fact, however, that in Plato's mind the gods
were inferior to the Ideas. The Sun, for instance, was held by Plato as a god; and yet in
his doctrine the Sun, who is a god, is a child
of the Good, which is not a god. In order to
understand Plato's own idea of a god, we must
first imagine some individual living being, similar to those we know from sensible experience;
but instead of imagining it as changeable,

the name of "god" attached by Plato to any Idea. In *Republic,* 508, it is said that the sun, whose soul is a god, is
the child of the Good, but it is not said that the Good is a
god. In *Phaedrus,* 247, Plato describes the "intangible
essence, visible only to mind" (Jowett trans., I, 252), then
Justice, Temperance, and Knowledge, as the heavenly objects of contemplation for "the divine Intelligence," but
the Intelligence alone is here called divine; its objects are
not called "gods." In *Phaedo,* 80, the soul is called "divine," in contradistinction to its body; and where Plato
adds (Jowett trans., I, 465) that "the soul is in the very
likeness of the divine, and immortal, and intellectual, and
uniform, and indissoluble, and unchangeable," even if it
had to be granted that he is here speaking of the Ideas,
not of the other gods, Plato would have simply said that
the Ideas are divine, not that they are gods. The identification of the Platonic Ideas with gods is still waiting for
its historical justification.

contingent, and mortal, we must conceive it as
intelligible, immutable, necessary, and eternal.
This is a god for Plato. In short, a Platonic
god is a living individual endowed with all the
fundamental attributes of an Idea. This is
the reason why a Platonic Idea can be more
divine than a god, and yet not be a god. If we
take man as a body quickened by a soul, man
is mortal and corruptible; hence he is not a
god. On the contrary, human souls are such
living individual beings as are of intelligible
nature and immortal in their own right; hence
the human souls are gods. There are many
gods higher than our own souls, but none of
them is an Idea. There are the Olympians,
whom Plato does not take too seriously, but
nevertheless preserves after purifying them of
their human weaknesses; after them come the
gods of the state; then the gods below, without
forgetting the demons or spirits, the heroes,
"and after them . . . the private and ances-
tral gods who are worshipped as the law pre-
scribes in the places which are sacred to
them."[24] Clearly enough, the world of Plato is

24. Plato, *Republic*, 717, Jowett trans., II, 488. The historical problem, classical in the world of Platonic scholar-
ship, whether or not the so-called "Creator" (or World-
Maker) of the *Timaeus* (28 and ff.) is an Idea, should not
even be asked. The "Creator" is a god working after the
pattern of the eternal Ideas; he is a god-maker of other
gods, such as the stars, the souls, and so on. Cf. *Laws*, X,
889, Jowett trans., II, 631.

no less full of gods than the world of Thales
or that of Homer; and his gods are just as
distinct from his philosophical principles as
an order of persons is distinct from an order
of things.

It is the presence of this world of divinities
in Plato's dialogues which confers upon his
doctrine its universally recognized religious
character. Plato's religion is not to be looked
for in the dialectical purification whereby the
philosopher frees himself from his body and
grows more and more comfortable to the intelligible Ideas. When a philosopher thus
reaches the intelligible world, he does not,
strictly speaking, divinize his soul: his soul is
a god in its own right. He does not even,
strictly speaking, immortalize his soul: his
soul is an indestructible life; it is immortal in
its own right. A philosopher is a human soul
which remembers its own divinity and behaves
as becomes a god. The true religion of Plato
consists in his feeling of adoration toward the
innumerable gods to whom men pray and
whom they invoke in their individual needs as
well as in the needs of their cities. As a philosopher Plato writes his *Timaeus;* as a religious man, Plato invokes the gods and the
goddesses of the world he is about to describe,
before beginning to descibe it.[25] Just like any

25. Plato, *Timaeus,* 27, Jowett trans., II, 12.

other man, Plato needs to feel himself sur-
rounded with personal powers which take care
of his own life and of his own destiny. Typically enough, the main attribute of a Platonic
god is to be a providence to man.[26] Owing to
the friendly presence of his divinities, Plato
does not feel himself alone in a chaotic desert
of inanimate things. "All things are full of
gods," Plato expressly repeats after Thales,
and he can never think too highly of his divine
protectors. "You have a low opinion of mankind, Stranger," Megillus says in the VII
Book of *Laws;* and the Athenian's answer is:
"Nay, Megillus, be not amazed, but forgive
me:—I was comparing them with the gods."[27]

This description of Plato's religious attitude not only clears up some aspects of his
doctrine but also enables us to grasp, at its
point of emergence, the philosophical notion
of god. Plato, who seems to have invented the
Ideas as a philosophical principle of explanation, did not invent the gods. They appear in
his doctrine as a legacy of Greek mythology,
and this is why they play so large a part in

26. Plato, *Laws,* X, 888, Jowett trans., II, 630. Cf. *ibid.,*
X, 899–907, II, 641–649. The conclusion of this text is
"that the Gods exist, and that they take care of men, and
that they can never be persuaded to do injustice." *Laws,*
X, 907, II, 649.

27. *Ibid.,* VII, 804, Jowett trans., II, 559.

Plato's myths. Time and again the philosopher reminds us that the belief of men in the
existence of the gods is a very ancient and
therefore a venerable one. This avowedly inherited belief however is susceptible of some
rational justification. And the way Plato jus-
tifies it is highly suggestive. Every time we
see a living thing and self-moving thing,
quickened from within by a spontaneous
power of operation, we can be sure that such a
thing has a soul; and since every soul is a god,
each living thing is inhabited by a god. Such
are, for instance, the sun and the other stars,
whose perpetual revolutions witness to the
presence in them of some divinity. In other
words, the soul is to Plato the very pattern
after which men have formed their notion of
god. Were it not for human souls, how could
you account for the spontaneous motion of
human bodies? But then, Plato adds, how are
you to account for the spontaneous motion of
the stars, unless you ascribe to each of them
some sort of soul? If you do, you must acknowledge at the same time that each and
every star is inhabited by a god.[28]

28. *Ibid.*, X, 899, II, 641. Cf. XII, 966–967, II, 700–702.
For a criticism of the fabulous mythology of Homer and
Hesiod, see *Republic*, II, 377–378, Jowett trans., I, 641–
642.

In his own objective and matter of fact manner, Aristotle has drawn from Plato's demonstration the lesson it teaches concerning the origin of our philosophical notion of god. Men, Aristotle says, have derived it from two sources: their own souls and the motion of the stars.[29] And if we remember the gods of Homer, it is at once apparent that Aristotle was right.

What makes Aristotle's metaphysics an epoch-making event in the history of natural theology is that in it the long delayed conjunction of the first philosophical principle with the notion of god became at last an accomplished fact. The prime mover of the Aristotelian universe is also its supreme god. And thus to become a god was an appreciable gain for the first philosophical principle and supreme cause of the world, but thus to become just so many philosophical principles was to prove a most perilous adventure for the whole family of the Greek gods. That the old Olympians had then to step out of the picture was a gain rather than a loss, not only to philoso-

29. Aristotle, "fragment 12," in *Aristotelis Opera* (Berlin, 1870), V, 1475–1476. In dreams and in divination, the soul seems to behave as if it were a god; as to the stars, their orderly motion suggests that there are causes of their motion and of their order. Each one of these causes is a god.

phy, but even to religion. The real danger,
for what was still going to be left of the gods,
was that of losing their very divinity.

The world of Aristotle is there, as something that has always been and always will be.
It is an eternally necessary and a necessarily
eternal world. The problem for us is therefore
not to know how it has come into being but to
understand what happens in it and consequently what it is. At the summit of the Aristotelian universe is not an Idea but a self-
subsisting and eternal Act of thinking. Let
us call it Thought: a divine self-thinking
Thought. Below it are the concentric heavenly spheres, each of which is eternally moved
by a distinct Intelligence, which itself is a distinct god. From the eternal motion of these
spheres the generation and corruption, that
is, the birth and death, of all earthly things
are eternally caused. Obviously, in such a doctrine, the theological interpretation of the
world is one with its philosophical and scientific explanation.[30] The only question is: Can
we still have a religion? The pure Act of the
self-thinking Thought eternally thinks of
itself, but never of us. The supreme god of
Aristotle has not made this world of ours; he

30. On the self-thinking Thought of Aristotle, see his
Metaphysics, Bk. XI, chaps. vii and ix.

does not even know it as distinct from himself, nor, consequently, can he take care of any one of the beings or things that are in it. It is true each human individual is endowed with a soul of his own, but this soul is no longer an immortal god like the Platonic soul; a physical form of a material and perishable body, the soul of man is doomed to perish with it. Perhaps we ought to love the god of Aristotle, but what would be the use, since this god himself does not love us? From time to time a few wise men succeed in sharing for a fleeting moment in the eternal beatitude of the divine contemplation. But even when philosophers succeed in descrying from afar the highest truth, their beatitude is a short-lived one, and philosophers are scarce. Truly wise men do not play at being gods; they rather aim to achieve the practical wisdom of moral and political life. God is in his heaven; it is up to men to take care of the world. With Aristotle, the Greeks had gained an indisputably rational theology, but they had lost their religion.

Once freed by the philosophers from the care of earthly things, the Greek gods seem to have renounced, once and for all, their former interest in man and his destiny. The popular gods of Greek mythology have never ceased to perform their religious functions, but the ra-

tionalized gods of the philosophers no longer
had any religious function to perform. In the
doctrine of Epicurus, for instance, the gods
are so many eternally subsisting material beings, whose perfect blessedness entails that
they should never worry about anything else,
particularly about men.[31] As to the great
Stoics, it is impossible to open their works
without meeting there, in practically every
chapter, the name of god. But what is their
god, if not fire, the material element out of
which this universe is made? Owing to it, the
world is one; an all-pervading harmony, or
sympathy, links together its parts, and each
of us is in it, as one of its many parts: "For
there is both one Universe, made up of all
things, and one God immanent in all things,
and one Substance, and one Law, one Reason
common to all intelligent creatures, and one
Truth." Since we find ourselves in the world
as in the City of Zeus, to love it is for us by
far the wisest course to follow.[32] Whether we
like it or not, however, we shall have to yield

31. On the survival of Aristotelian elements in the Epi-
curean notion of the gods, see the excellent remarks of
A. J. Festugière, O.P., *op. cit.*, p. 63.

32. *The Communings with Himself of Marcus Aurelius,*
text and trans. by C. R. Haines (London, 1916), Loeb
Classical Library. Cf. Bk. VII, 9, p. 169 and Bk. IV, 23,
p. 81.

to the necessity of its laws: "The World-Cause
is a torrent," Marcus Aurelius says, "it sweeps
everything along."[33] And again: "The Nature
of the Whole felt impelled to the creation of a
Universe; but now either all that comes into
being does so by a natural sequence, or even
the most paramount things, toward which the
ruling Reason of the Universe feels an impulse of its own, are devoid of intelligence.
Recollect this and thou wilt face many an ill
with more serenity."[34]

It has been said of Marcus Aurelius that he
has not had the god he deserved. It might still
more truly be said that Marcus Aurelius has
had no god at all. His piety toward god is but
a wise resignation to what he knows to be inevitable. "A little while and thou wilt have
forgotten everything, a little while and everything will have forgotten thee."[35] These words
of the great Stoic also are the last words of
Greek wisdom, and they clearly mark the fail-

33. *Ibid.*, Bk. IX, 29, pp. 247–248.
34. *Ibid.*, Bk. VII, 75, p. 197.
35. *Ibid.*, Bk. VII, 22, p. 173. Even in Marcus Aurelius,
the gods are still present as friendly powers who take
care of men and do their best to protect them from evil
(see, for instance, Bk. II, 11, pp. 32–35); but the gods of
Marcus Aurelius play an infinitesimal part in his doctrine; even their good will does not inspire him with any
more cheerful feeling than an almost desperate resignation.

ure of the Greeks to build up an all-compre-
hensive philosophical explanation of the world
without at the same time losing their religion.
In the light of what precedes, the reason for
their failure is at hand. A Greek philosophical
interpretation of the world is an explanation
of what natures are, by what a certain nature
is; in other words, the Greeks have consistently tried to explain all things by means of
one or several principles themselves considered as things. Now, men can be preached into
worshiping any living being, from a wholly
imaginary one like Zeus to a wholly ridiculous
one like the Golden Calf. Provided only it be
somebody or something which they can mistake for somebody, they may eventually worship it. What men cannot possibly bring themselves to do is to worship a thing. When Greek
philosophy came to an end, what was sorely
needed for progress in natural theology was
progress in metaphysics. Such philosophical
progress was to be made as early as the fourth
century A.D.; but, curiously enough, metaphysics was to make it under the influence of
religion.

II

GOD AND CHRISTIAN PHILOSOPHY

WHILE the Greek philosophers were wondering what place to assign to their gods in a philosophically intelligible world, the Jews had already found the God who was to provide philosophy with an answer to its own question. Not a God imagined by poets or discovered by any thinker as an ultimate answer to his metaphysical problems, but one who had revealed Himself to the Jews, told them His name, and explained to them His nature, in so far at least as His nature can be understood by men.

The first character of the Jewish God was his unicity: "Hear, O Israel: the Lord our God is one Lord."[1] Impossible to achieve a more far-reaching revolution in fewer words or in a simpler way. When Moses made this statement, he was not formulating any metaphysical principle to be later supported by rational justification. Moses was simply speaking as an inspired prophet and defining for the benefit of the Jews what was henceforth to be the sole object of their worship. Yet, es-

1. Deuteronomy 6.4.

sentially religious as it was, this statement contained the seed of a momentous philosophical revolution, in this sense at least, that should any philosopher, speculating at any time about the first principle and cause of the world, hold the Jewish God to be the true God, he would be necessarily driven to identify his supreme philosophical cause with God. In other words, whereas the difficulty was, for a Greek philosopher, to fit a plurality of gods into a reality which he conceived as one, any follower of the Jewish God would know at once that, whatever the nature of reality itself may be said to be, its religious principle must of necessity coincide with its philosophical principle. Each of them being one, they are bound to be the same and to provide men with one and the same explanation of the world.

When the existence of this one true God was proclaimed by Moses to the Jews, they never thought for a moment that their Lord could be some thing. Obviously, their Lord was somebody. Besides, since he was the God of the Jews, they already knew Him; and they knew Him as the Lord God of their fathers, the God of Abraham, the God of Isaac, and the God of Jacob. Time and again, their God had proved to them that He was taking care of His people; their relations with

Him had always been personal relations, that is, relations between persons and another person; the only thing they still wanted to know about Him was what to call Him. As a matter of fact, Moses himself did not know the name of the one God; but he knew that the Jews would ask him for it; and instead of engaging upon deep metaphysical meditations to discover the true name of God, he took a typically religious short cut. Moses simply asked God about His name, saying to Him: "Lo, I shall go to the children of Israel, and say to them: The God of your fathers hath sent me to you. If they should say to me: What is His name? What shall I say to them? God said to Moses: I AM WHO AM. He said: Thus shalt thou say to the children of Israel: HE WHO IS, hath sent me to you."[2] Hence the universally known name of the Jewish God— Yahweh, for Yahweh means "He who is."

Here again historians of philosophy find themselves confronted with this to them always unpalatable fact: a nonphilosophical statement which has since become an epoch-making statement in the history of philosophy. The Jewish genius was not a philosophical genius; it was a religious one. Just as the Greeks are our masters in philosophy, the

2. Exodus 3.13–14.

Jews are our masters in religion. So long as the Jews kept their own religious revelation to themselves, nothing happened to philosophy. But owing to the preaching of the Gospel the God of the Jews ceased to be the private God of an elect race and became the universal God of all men. Any Christian convert who was at all familiar with Greek philosophy was then bound to realize the metaphysical import of his new religious belief. His philosophical first principle had to be one with his religious first principle, and since the name of his God was "I am," any Christian philosopher had to posit "I am" as his first principle and supreme cause of all things, even in philosophy. To use our own modern terminology, let us say that a Christian's philosophy is "existential" in its own right.

This point was of such importance that even the earliest Christian thinkers did not fail to see it. When the first educated Greeks became converts to Christianity, the Olympian gods of Homer had already been discredited as mere mythical imaginings through the repeated criticism of the philosophers. But those very philosophers had no less completely discredited themselves by giving to the world the spectacle of their endless contradictions. Even those who were the greatest among

them, taken at their very best, had never succeeded in correctly stating what they at least
should have held to be the supreme cause of all
things. Plato, for instance, had clearly seen
that the ultimate philosophical explanation
for all that which is should ultimately rest,
not within those elements of reality that are
always being generated and therefore never
really are, but with something which, because
it has no generation, truly is, or exists. Now,
as has been pointed out by the unknown author of the *Hortatory Address to the Greeks*
as early as the third century A.D. what Plato
had said was almost exactly what the Christians themselves were saying, "saving only the
difference of the article. For Moses said: *He
who is*, and Plato: *That which is*." And it is
quite true that "either of the expressions seems
to apply to the existence of God."[3] If God is
"He who is," he also is "that which is," because to be somebody is also to be something.
Yet the converse is not true, for to be somebody is much more than to be something.

We are here at the dividing line between
Greek thought and Christian thought, that is

3. *Hortatory Address to the Greeks,* chap. xxii, published among the works of Justin Martyr, in *The Ante-
Nicene Fathers* (Buffalo, 1885), I, 272. Cf. E. Gilson,
L'Esprit de la philosophie médiévale (Paris, J. Vrin,
1932), I, 227, n. 7.

to say, between Greek philosophy and Christian philosophy. Taken in itself, Christianity was not a philosophy. It was the essentially religious doctrine of the salvation of men through Christ. Christian philosophy arose at the juncture of Greek philosophy and of the Jewish-Christian religious revelation, Greek philosophy providing the technique for a rational explanation of the world, and the Jewish-Christian revelation providing religious beliefs of incalculable philosophical import. What is perhaps the key to the whole history of Christian philosophy and, in so far as modern philosophy bears the mark of Christian thought, to the history of modern philosophy itself, is precisely the fact that, from the second century A.D. on, men have had to use a Greek philosophical technique in order to express ideas that had never entered the head of any Greek philosopher.

This was by no means an easy task. The Greeks had never gone further than the natural theology of Plato and of Aristotle, not on account of intellectual weakness on their part, but, on the contrary, because both Plato and Aristotle had pushed their investigations almost as far as human reason alone can take us. By positing, as the supreme cause of all that which is, somebody who is, and of whom

the very best that can be said is that "He is,"
Christian revelation was establishing existence
as the deepest layer of reality as well as the
supreme attribute of the divinity. Hence, in
so far as the world itself was concerned, the
entirely new philosophical problem of its very
existence, and the still deeper one whose
formula runs thus: What is it to exist? As
Prfoessor J. B. Muller-Thym aptly remarks,
where a Greek simply asks: What is nature?
a Christian rather asks: What is being?[4]

The first epoch-making contact between
Greek philosophical speculation and Christian
religious belief took place when, already a
convert to Christianity, the young Augustine
began to read the works of some Neo-Plato-
nists, particularly the *Enneads* of Plotinos.[5]

4. J. B. Muller-Thym, *On the University of Being in
Meister Eckhart of Hochheim* (New York, Sheed and
Ward, 1939), p. 2.

5. For a good introduction to the many interpretations of this historical fact, see Charles Boyer, S.J., *La
Formation de saint Augustin* (Paris, Beauchesne, 1920).
An exactly opposite view is maintained by P. Alfaric,
L'Évolution intellectuelle de saint Augustin (Paris,
Nourry, 1918). The very nature of the problem entails
psychological hypotheses which cannot be either historically demonstrated or historically refuted. I feel personally convinced that the views of C. Boyer on the
question are fundamentally sound, but nobody should
subscribe to them before carefully weighing the arguments set forward by Alfaric in support of his own interpretation.

Augustine found there, not the pure philosophy of Plato, but an original synthesis of Plato, Aristotle, and the Stoics. Moreover, even where he borrowed from Plato, Plotinos had identified the Idea of Good, as described in the *Republic*, with that other puzzling principle, the One, which makes its late appearance in Plato's *Parmenides*. The very conclusion of this dialogue seems to have provided Plotinos with the keystone of his own metaphysical system: "Then were we to say in a word: if the one is not, nothing is, should we be right?— Most assuredly." And indeed, if the One is that without which nothing else could be, the existence of the whole world must of necessity depend upon some eternally subsisting Unity.

Let us then imagine, with Plotinos, a first principle whom we will call the One. Strictly speaking, he is unnamable because he cannot be described. Any attempt at expressing him must of necessity result in a judgment, and since a judgment is made up of several terms, we cannot say what the One is without turning his unity into some sort of multiplicity, that is, without destroying it. Let us say then that he is the One, not as a number that can enter the composition of other numbers, nor as a synthesis of other numbers, but as the self-subsisting unity whence all multiplicity follows without affecting in the least its absolute simplicity. From the fecundity of the One a second principle is born, inferior to the first, yet eternally subsisting like the One and, after him, the cause of all that comes after him. His name is the Intellect. Unlike the One, the Intellect is the self-subsisting knowledge of all that is intelligible. Since he himself is both the knowing subject and the known object, he is as near being the One as it is possible to be; yet since he is affected by the duality of subject and object inherent in all knowledge, he is not the One; consequently he is inferior to him.

Among the attributes which belong to the Intellect, two are of particular importance for a correct understanding of our historical problem. Conceived as an eternally subsisting cognition of all that which is intelligible, the Intellect of Plotinos is, by definition, the locus of all the Ideas. They are in him as a multiple intelligible unity; they are eternally sharing in the fecundity which he himself owes to the fecundity of the One; in short, the Intellect is big with all that multiplicity of individual and distinct beings which eternally flow from him. In this sense, he is a god and the father of all the other gods.

A second characteristic of the Intellect, much harder to grasp than the preceding one, is perhaps still more important. When can we say of anything: It is? As soon as, by an act of understanding, we apprehend it as distinct from something else. In other words, so long as nothing is actually understood, nothing is; which amounts to saying that being first appears in, by, and with this Intellect, who is the second principle in Plotinos' philosophy. These are the two supreme causes of the Plotinian universe: at the top, the One of Plato's *Parmenides;* immediately below him, and born of him, the self-thinking Thought of Aristotle, whom Plotinos calls the Nous, or Intellect, and whom he conceives as the locus of Plato's Ideas. Such also were the main data of the problem which Augustine boldly undertook to solve: how to express the God of Christianity in terms borrowed from the philosophy of Plotinos?

If we look at this problem as historians, and view it through fifteen centuries of history, our first impulse is to declare that such a problem was not susceptible of a satisfactory solution. Perhaps it was not. But we should remember that the creations of the human mind do not obey the analytical laws which

preside over their historical explanations.
What appears to us as a problem fraught with
tremendous difficulties was never perceived by
Augustine as a problem; the only thing he
was ever aware of was its solution.

Generations after generations of historians
have pondered over this extraordinary and,
in a way, inexplicable phenomenon. Here is a
young convert to Christianity who, for the
first time in his life, reads the *Enneads* of Plotinos, and what he sees there at once is the
Christian God himself, with all his essential
attributes. Who is the One, if not God the
Father, the first person of the Christian
Trinity? And who is the Nous, or Intellect, if
not the second person of the Christian Trinity,
that is, the Word, exactly as he appears at the
beginning of the Gospel of Saint John? "And
therein I read, not indeed in the same words,
but to the selfsame effect, enforced by many
and divers reasons, that: In the beginning was
the Word, and the Word was with God, and
the Word was God. All things were made by
Him; and without Him was not any thing
made that was made."[6] In short, as soon as
Augustine read the *Enneads*, he found there

6. Saint Augustine, *Confessions,* Bk. VII, chap. ix, n.
13, trans. by the Rev. Marcus Dods, in "The Works of
Aurelius Augustine" (Edinburgh, 1876), XIV, 152–153.

the three essentially Christian notions of God
the Father, of God the Word, and of the
creation.

That Augustine found them there is an in-
controvertible fact. That they were not there
is a hardly more controvertible fact. To go at
once to the fundamental reason why they
could not possibly be there, let us say that the
world of Plotinos and the world of Christianity
are strictly incomparable; no single point in
the one can be matched with any single point
in the other one, for the fundamental reason
that their metaphysical structure is essentially different. Plotinos was living in the
third century A.D.; yet his philosophical
thought remained wholly foreign to Christianity. His world is a Greek philosophical
world, made up of natures whose operations
are strictly determined by their essences. Even
the One of Plotinos, whom we can hardly refrain from designating as a He, exists and
operates after the manner of an It. If we compare him to the rest, the One, or Good, is absolutely free, because all the rest depends upon
him for its existence, whereas he himself,
being the first principle, does not depend upon
anything else. Taken in himself, on the contrary, the One is strictly determined by his
own nature; not only the One is what he has

to be, but he acts as he has to act on account of what he necessarily is. Hence the typically Greek aspect of the Plotinian universe as a natural, eternal, and necessary generation of all things by the One. Everything eternally flows from him as a radiation which he himself does not even know, because he is above thought, above being, above the duality of being and thought. In Plotinos' own words: "As to the unbegotten principle, who has nothing above him, who is eternally what he is, what reason might he have to think?"[7]

To Plotinos' question, let our answer be: No reason whatsoever; but let us immediately add that this alone is a sufficient reason why the god of Plotinos cannot possibly be the Christian God nor the world of Plotinos a Christian world. The Plotinian universe is typically Greek in this, that in it God is neither the supreme reality nor the ultimate principle of intelligibility. Hence this metaphysically momentous consequence, that the dividing line between the first cause and all the rest does not coincide in a philosophy of the One and in a philosophy of being. Since nothing can beget itself, what the One begets

7. Plotinos, *Enneads,* VI, 7, 37, in "Complete Works," trans. by Kenneth Sylvan Guthrie (Alpine, N. J., Platonist Press), III, 762.

has to be other than the One; consequently, it must of necessity be multiple. This applies even to the Intellect, who is the highest Plotinian god. The Plotinian dividing line thus cuts off the One, who is the only unbegotten principle, from all the begotten multiplicity, that is to say, from all the rest. In all the rest are to be found the Intellect, who is the first god, followed by the supreme Soul, who is the second god, then all the other gods including the human souls. In other words, while there is a radical difference of nature between the One, or Good, and all that which, because it is not the One, is multiple, there are but differences of degrees between all that which is not the One, and yet is, or exists. We ourselves belong in the same metaphysical class as the Intellect and the supreme Soul; we are gods just as they are, begotten from the One just as they are, and inferior to them, in proportion to our respective degrees of multiplicity, as they themselves are inferior to the One.

Not so in a Christian metaphysics of being, where the supreme principle is a God whose true name is "He who is." A pure Act of existing, taken as such and without any limitation, necessarily is all that which it is possible to be. We cannot even say that such a God has knowledge, or love, or anything else; he is it in his own right, for the very reason that, were he not everything and anything that it is possible to be, he could be called "He who is" but with some added qualification. If, as is part of Christian faith, such a God begets in virtue of his infinite fecundity, he must beget somebody else, that is another person, but not something else, that is another God. Otherwise, there would be two absolute acts of existing, each of which would include the totality of being, which is absurd. If, on the other hand, such a God actually is, or exists, his self-sufficiency is so perfect that there can be no necessity for anything else to exist. Nothing can be added to him; nothing can be subtracted from him; and since nothing can share in his being without at once being himself; "He who is" can eternally enjoy the fullness of his own perfection, of his own beatitude, without needing to grant existence to anybody else, or to anything whatsoever.

Yet it is a fact that there is something which is not God. Men, for instance, are not such an eternal act of absolute existence. There are therefore some beings that are radically different from God at least in this that, unlike him, they might not have existed, and still may, at a certain time, cease to exist. Thus to be, or exist, is not at all to be, or exist, as God him-

self is, or exists. It is therefore not to be an inferior sort of god; rather, it is not to be a god
at all. The only possible explanation for the
presence of such finite and contingent beings
is that they have been freely given existence
by "Him who is," and not as parcels of his
own existence, which, because it is absolute
and total, is also unique, but as finite and par-
tial imitations of what He himself eternally is
in his own right. This act whereby "He who
is" causes to exist something that, of itself, is
not, is what is called, in Christian philosophy,
"creation." Whence there follows, that whereas
all that which the Christian God begets must
of necessity share in the oneness of God, all
that which does not share in his oneness must
of necessity be not begotten but created.

Such is, in fact, the Christian world of
Saint Augustine. On the one side, God, one
in the Trinity of a single, self-existing substance; on the other side, all that which, because it has but a received existence, is not
God. Unlike the Plotinian dividing line which
we have seen running between the One and all
that is begotten by the One, the Christian dividing line runs between God, including his
own begotten Word, and all that is created by
God. As one among God's creatures, man finds
himself therein excluded from the order of the

divine. Between "Him who is" and ourselves,
there is the infinite metaphysical chasm which
separates the complete self-sufficiency of His
own existence from the intrinsic lack of necessity of our own existence. Nothing can bridge
such a chasm, save a free act of the divine will
only. This is why, from the time of Saint
Augustine up to our own days, human reason
has been up against the tremendously difficult
task of reaching a transcendent God whose
pure act of existing is radically distinct from
our own borrowed existence. How can man,
who out of himself is not, living in a world of
things which out of themselves are not, reach,
by means of reason alone, "Him who is"?
Such is, to a Christian, the fundamental problem of natural theology.

In his effort to solve this problem, Augustine had nothing to help him but the philosophical technique of Plato in the revised edition of Plotinos. Here again, the philosophical
eagerness of the Christian convert took him
beyond the data of the problem straight to its
solution. Interpreting Plato's doctrine of
reminiscence, Plotinos had described dialectics as an effort of the human soul to rid itself
of all material images so as to contemplate the
intelligible Ideas in the light of the first Intellect, who is the supreme god. Was not this

exactly what Saint John himself had, if not philosophically established, at least clearly suggested in the first chapter of his gospel? When Plotinos and Saint John thus met in the mind of Augustine, their combination was instantaneous. Reading the gospel into Plotinos' *Enneads*, he found there that the soul of man, though it "bears witness of the light," yet itself "is not that light; but the Word of God, being God, is that true light that lighteth every man that cometh into the world."[8] Why should not men use this constant presence of the divine light in their souls as an always open way to the Christian God?

This is precisely what Augustine did, or, at least, what he tried to do, for the task proved to be a much more difficult one than he himself had imagined. In inheriting the philosophical world of Plato, Augustine had fallen heir to Plato's man. Now, man, as Plato conceived him, was not the substantial unity of body and soul; he was essentially a soul. Instead of saying that man *has* a soul, we should therefore say that man *is* a particular soul, that is to say, an intelligent, intelligible, and eternally

8. Saint John, 1. 7–9. Cf. Saint Augustine, *op. cit.,* Bk. VII, chap. ix, n. 13, English trans., p. 154. The text of Saint John directly applies to the problem of human salvation through Christ.

living substance, which, though it now happens to be conjoined to a body, has always existed before it and is ultimately destined to outlive it. In Plato's own words, man is "a soul using a body,"[9] but he is no more his body than a worker is the tools he uses or than any one of us is his own garments.

By accepting this definition of man, Augustine was putting himself in an exceedingly awkward philosophical position. In Plato's doctrine, and still more clearly in that of Plotinos, to be a purely intelligible, living, and immortal substance was exactly to be a god. Human souls then are just so many gods. When a man philosophizes and, discarding his body, focuses his mind upon intelligible truth, he simply behaves like a god who remembers to be a god. Rightly to philosophize then is nothing else, for each and every one of us, than to behave as becomes the god which each and every one of us actually is. True, we all are but individual Intelligences radiated by the supreme Intellect, and therefore by the One. For this very reason, just as we are by and in the One, we also know, and contem-

9. Plato, *Alcibiades,* 129e–130c. Saint Augustine, *De Moribus ecclesiae,* Bk. I, chap. xxvii, p. 52; *Patrologia Latina,* Vol. XXXII, col. 1332. Cf. É. Gilson, *Introduction à l'étude de saint Augustin* (Paris, J. Vrin, 1929), p. 55.

plate, by and in the light of the supreme Intellect who eternally emanates from the One.
Yet, when all is said and done, we nevertheless
are so many gods, lesser gods as we may be,
patiently working our way back into the com-
pany of our fellow gods. Dialectics, as Plato
and Plotinos understood it, was but the method
which enables man to achieve a sort of philosophical salvation, by progressively raising
him to the full awareness of his own divinity.
A god may eventually forget himself but he
cannot possibly stand in need of being saved.[10]

This is the fundamental reason why Saint
Augustine has found it so hard to reach the
Christian God by means of methods borrowed
from Plato and Plotinos. To him, as to them,
all that was immaterial, intelligible, and true
was divine in its own right; but, whereas, in
Plato's philosophy, man was naturally entitled
to the possession of truth as a divinity is entitled to the possession of things divine, he
could no longer appear as entitled to it in a
Christian philosophy where, metaphysically

10. On this problem, see the extremely important analy-
ses of Marcel de Corte, *Aristôte et Plotin* (Paris, Desclée
de Brouwer, 1935), chap. iii, "La Purification plotini-
enne," pp. 177–227, and chap. vi, "La Dialectique de
Plotin," pp. 229–290. These two essays are probably the
deepest existing introductions to the method and spirit of
the doctrine of Plotinos.

speaking,[11] man in no way belongs in the divine order. Hence this important consequence, that man was bound to appear to Augustine as a creature endowed with something that was divine in its own right. If truth is divine, and if man is not a god, man should not be possessed of truth. In fact, however, man is; consequently, the only conceivable way for Augustine to account for the paradoxical presence of intelligible truth, which is divine, in man, who is not a god, was to consider man

11. I beg to stress the words "metaphysically speaking," in order to make clear the radical difference there is between the order of metaphysics and the order of religion. As a Christian, any man can be "deified" through grace, because grace is a sharing in the life of God. Thus understood, grace is supernatural in its own right. So also is the whole sacramental order, as clearly appears from the well-known prayer of the Ordinary of the Mass, which I beg to quote in full because of its perfect clarity: "O God, who in creating human nature hast wonderfully dignified it, and still more wonderfully reformed it; grant by the mystery of this Water and Wine, *we may be made partakers of His divine nature,* who vouchsafed to become partaker of our human nature, namely, Jesus Christ, our Lord, Thy Son, who with Thee, livest and reignest, in the unity of the Holy Ghost, God, world without end. Amen." The man of Plato stood in no need of being made partaker of the divinity, because he himself was a god; hence, for Augustine, the necessity of stripping the man of Plato of what made him god, namely, his natural aptness to know truth. We will find Thomas Aquinas confronted with the contrary difficulty, namely, that of turning the eminently natural man of Aristotle into a being susceptible of deification.

as knowing in the permanent light of a supremely intelligible and self-subsisting truth,
that is, in the light of God.

Time and again, under a variety of different forms, Augustine has attempted the same
demonstration of the existence of God as the
only conceivable cause of the presence of
truth in the human mind. His God is the intelligible sun whose light shines upon human
reason and enables it to know truth; he is the
inner master who teaches man from within;
his eternal and unchangeable ideas are the
supreme rules whose influence submits our
reason to the necessity of divine truth. As
demonstrations, the arguments of Saint Augustine are very effective. Granting that
truth is superhuman and divine in its own
right, the bare fact that man knows truth con-
clusively proves the existence of God. But
why should we grant Augustine that truth is
a more than human object of knowledge? The
only reason why he himself thought so was a
merely accidental one. Augustine's implicit
reasoning seems to have run as follows: Plato
and Plotinos consider man as a god because
man is possessed of truth; now man is em-
phatically not a god; hence man cannot possibly be possessed of truth. Taken in itself,

such an argument is perfectly correct; it
would even be a perfectly conclusive one if it
were true to say that truth is too good a thing
to be considered as naturally attainable by
man.

What happened to Saint Augustine is only
too clear. An unsurpassed exponent of Christian wisdom, he never had the philosophy of
his theology. The God of Augustine is the
true Christian God, of whose pure Act of existing nothing better can be said than: He is;
but when Augustine undertakes to describe
existence in philosophical terms, he at once
falls back upon the Greek identification of
being with the notions of immateriality, intelligibility, immutability, and unity. Every
such thing is divine; since truth is such, truth
is divine. Immaterial, intelligible, and immutable, truth belongs in the order of that which
truly is, or exists. Consequently, it belongs to
God. Similarly the God of Augustine is the
true creator of all things; but when it comes
to defining creation, Augustine naturally
understands it in accordance with his own notion of being. To create is to give being, and
since to be is to be both intelligible and one,
Augustine understands creation as the divine
gift of that sort of existence which consists in
rhythm, numbers, forms, beauty, order, and

unity.[12] Like all Christians, but unlike the Greeks, Augustine has a quite clear notion of what it is to create something "out of nothing." It is to make it to be. What still remains Greek in Augustine's thought is his very notion of what it is to be. His ontology, or science of being, is an "essential" rather than an "existential" one. In other words, it exhibits a marked tendency to reduce the existence of a thing to its essence, and to answer the question: What is it for a thing to be? by saying: It is to be that which it is.

A most sensible answer indeed, but perhaps not the deepest conceivable one in philosophy, and certainly not a perfectly suitable one for a Christian philosopher speculating on a world created by the Christian God. For reasons which I will later try to make clear, it was

12. On the metaphysical constituents of concrete existence, see Emmanuel Chapman, *Saint Augustine's Philosophy of Beauty* (New York, Sheed and Ward, 1939), chap. ii, pp. 13–44. The Platonic character of the Augustinian notion of creation has been stressed, and perhaps slightly overstressed, by A. Gardeil, *La Structure mystique de l'âme* (Paris, Gabalda, 1929), Appendix II, vol. II, 319–320. After rereading my own criticism of A. Gardeil's interpretation (in *Introduction à l'étude de saint Augustin,* p. 258, n. 8), I have reached the conclusion that what Gardeil had in mind when he wrote these pages was fundamentally true; yet I myself was not altogether wrong. Augustine had a clear idea of what it is to create, but he never reached a wholly existential notion of being.

not easy to go beyond Saint Augustine, because the limit he had reached was the limit of
Greek ontology itself, and therefore just
about the very limit which the human mind
can reach in matters of metaphysics. When,
nine centuries after the death of Saint Augustine, a new and decisive progress in natural
theology was made, its occasional cause was
the discovery of another Greek metaphysical
universe by another Christian theologian.
This time the metaphysical universe was that
of Aristotle, and the name of the theologian
was Thomas Aquinas.

"The religious side of Plato's thought,"
Gilbert Murray rightly says, "was not revealed in its full power till the time of Plotinos in the third century A.D.: that of Aristotle, one might say without undue paradox,
not till its exposition by Aquinas in the thir-
teenth."[13] Let us add only this, that the "explanation" of Aristotle by Thomas Aquinas
might perhaps be more justly called its meta-
morphosis in the light of Christian revelation.
The self-thinking Thought of Aristotle has
certainly become an essential element of the
natural theology of Saint Thomas Aquinas,
but not without first undergoing the meta-

13. Gilbert Murray, *Five Stages of Greek Religion*
(New York, Columbia University Press, 1925), p. 17.

physical transformation that turned him into
the *Qui est*, or "He who is" of the Old Testament.[14]

Why, Saint Thomas asks, do we say that
Qui est is the most proper name among all
those that can be given to God? And his answer is because it signifies "to be" : *ipsum esse*.
But what is it to be? In answering this most
difficult of all metaphysical questions, we must
carefully distinguish between the meaning of
two words which are both different and yet
intimately related: *ens*, or "being," and *esse*,
or "to be." To the question: What is being?
the correct answer is: Being is that which is,
or exists. If, for instance, we ask this same
question with regard to God, the correct answer would be: The being of God is an infinite
and boundless ocean of substance.[15] But *esse*,
or "to be," is something else and much harder
to grasp because it lies more deeply hidden in
the metaphysical structure of reality. The
word "being," as a noun, designates some substance; the word "to be"—or *esse*—is a verb,

14. Saint Thomas Aquinas, *Summa theologica*, Pars I,
qu. 13, art. 11, *Sed contra*. On the Thomistic identification
of God with Being, see É. Gilson, *The Spirit of Mediaeval
Philosophy* (New York, Scribners, 1936), chap. iii, pp.
42–63.

15. This formula is quoted from John Damascene by
Saint Thomas Aquinas, *op. cit.*, Pars I, qu. 13, art. 11,
Resp.

because it designates an act. To understand this is also to reach, beyond the level of essence, the deeper level of existence. For it is quite true to say that all that which is a substance must of necessity have also both an essence and an existence. In point of fact, such is the natural order followed by our rational knowledge: we first conceive certain beings, then we define their essences, and last we affirm their existences by means of a judgment. But the metaphysical order of reality is just the reverse of the order of human knowledge: what first comes into it is a certain act of existing which, because it is *this* particuar act of existing, circumscribes at once a certain essence and causes a certain substance to come into being. In this deeper sense, "to be" is the primitive and fundamental act by virtue of which a certain being actually is, or exists. In Saint Thomas' own words: *dictur esse ipse actus essentiae*[16]—"to be" is the very act whereby an essence is.

A world where "to be" is the act par excel-

16. Saint Thomas Aquinas, in I. *Sent.,* dist. 33, qu. 1, art. 1, ad 1ᵐ. Cf. *Quaestiones disputatae: De Potentia,* qu. VII, art. 2, ad 9. This existential notion of being is discussed in É. Gilson, *Réalisme thomiste et critique de la connaissance* (Paris, J. Vrin, 1939), chap. viii, esp. pp. 220–222. For a general comparison between the God of Aristotle and the God of Saint Thomas Aquinas, see the penetrating essay of Anton C. Pegis, *Saint Thomas and*

lence, the act of all acts, is also a world
wherein, for each and every thing, existence is
the original energy whence flows all that which
deserves the name of being. Such an existential world can be accounted for by no other
cause than a supremely existential God. The
strange thing is that, historically speaking,
things seem to have worked the other way
around. Philosophers have not inferred the
supreme existentiality of God from any previ-
ous knowledge of the existential nature of
things; on the contrary, the self-revelation of
the existentiality of God has helped philosophers toward the realization of the existential
nature of things. In other words, philosophers
were not able to reach, beyond essences, the
existential energies which are their very
causes, until the Jewish-Christian Revelation
had taught them that "to be" was the proper
name of the Supreme Beisg. The decisive

the *Greeks* (Milwaukee, Marquette University Press
1939). For a comparison between the God of Augustine
and the God of Thomas Aquinas, see A. Gardeil, *La
Structure de l'âme et l'expérience mystique* (Paris, Gabalda, 1927), Appendix II, vol. II, 313–325. The extreme
simplicity of the notion of existence and the impossibility
of our conceptualizing it have been stressed by J. Maritain, *Sept leçons sur l'Être (1932–33)* (Paris, Téqui), pp.
98–99. These characteristics of "to be" probably account
for the fact that, as will be seen in Chapter IV, many
modern scientists consider the existence of a thing the
most negligible of all its properties.

progress achieved by metaphysics in the light of Christian faith has not been to realize that there must be a first being, cause of being in all things. The greatest among the Greeks already knew it. When, for instance, Aristotle was positing his first self-thinking Thought as the supreme being, he certainly conceived it as a pure Act and as an infinitely powerful energy; still, his god was but the pure Act of a Thought. This infinitely powerful actuality of a self-thinking principle most certainly deserves to be called a pure Act, but it was a pure Act in the order of knowing, not in that of existence. Now nothing can give what it has not. Because the supreme Thought of Aristotle was not "He who is," it could not give existence: hence the world of Aristotle was not a created world. Because the supreme Thought of Aristotle was not the pure Act of existing, its self-knowledge did not entail the knowledge of all being, both actual and possible: the god of Aristotle was not a providence; he did not even know a world which he did not make and which he could not possibly have made because he was the thought of a Thought, nor did he know the self-awareness of "Him who is."

I would not like to minimize the philosophical indebtedness of Thomas Aquinas to Aris-

totle. He himself would not forgive me for
making him guilty of such an ingratitude. As
a philosopher, Thomas Aquinas was not a
pupil of Moses, but of Aristotle, to whom he
owed his method, his principles, up to even his
all-important notion of the fundamental actuality of being. My only point is that a decisive
metaphysical progress or, rather, a true metaphysical revolution was achieved when somebody began to translate all the problems concerning being from the language of essences
into that of existences. From its earliest origins, metaphysics had always obscurely aimed
at becoming existential; from the time of Saint
Thomas Aquinas it has always been so, and to
such an extent that metaphysics has regularly
lost its very existence every time it has lost its
existentiality.

The metaphysics of Thomas Aquinas was,
and it still remains, a climax in the history of
natural theology. No wonder then that it was
so soon followed by an anticlimax. Human
reason feels at home in a world of things,
whose essences and laws it can grasp and define in terms of concepts; but shy and ill at
ease in a world of existences, because to exist
is an act, not a thing. And we know it but too
well. Every time a lecturer begins a sentence
by saying: "As a matter of fact," you know at

once that the man is at his wit's end. Granting
that something is, he can tell you a great deal
concerning that which it is; what he cannot do
is to account for the very existence of the
thing. How could he, if existence is a principle, and the innermost first principle of what
the thing is? When dealing with facts as facts,
or with things that happen as mere happen-
ings, our *ultima ratio* always is and that's
that. Obviously, to ask us to view the universe
as a world of particular existential acts all related to a supreme and absolute Self-Existence is to stretch the power of our essentially
conceptual reason almost to the breaking
point. We know that we must do it, but we
wonder if we can, because we are not sure that
the thing can be done at all.

This, at least, is a point about which several among the successors of Thomas Aquinas
have entertained grave doubts. Themselves
Christian theologians, and sometimes very
great ones, they had no hesitations concerning
the true name of the true God. Their real
difficulty was, granting that God is "He who
is," can such a God be attained by means of
philosophical reason alone, unaided by Revelation? A perfectly relevant question indeed.
After all, these theologians knew full well that
philosophers had never thought of giving God

such a name until they had learned it from
Moses, who himself had learned it from God.
Hence the marked tendency, even in such a
great metaphysician as Duns Scotus, to question the possibility of human reason's reaching, by means of philosophy alone, the absolutely existing and absolutely all-powerful
Christian God.[17]

The reason for this hesitancy is simple. The
human mind feels shy before a reality of which
it can form no proper concept. Such, precisely, is existence. It is hard for us to realize
that "I am" is an active verb. It is perhaps
still more difficult for us to see that "it is"
ultimately points out, not that which the thing
is, but the primitive existential act which

17. The existential character of being has been power-
fully stressed by Duns Scotus; cf. Parthenius Minges,
I. Duns Scoti Doctrina philosophica et theologica (Fi-
renze, Quaracchi, 1930), I, 14–17. What is peculiar to his
own theology is a marked tendency to make the Christian
God, taken qua Christian God, unknowable to natural
reason unaided by faith. Moreover, it would prove interesting to investigate into the Scotist notion of created
existence. According to him, "the essence and its existence in creatures are to each other as a quiddity to its
mode" (op. cit., pp. 16–17). The primacy of essence, which
makes existence to be but one of its "accidents," appears
in the doctrine of Duns Scotus as a remnant of the Pla-
tonism anterior to Thomas Aquinas. In a straight existential metaphysics, it would be much more correct to
speak of the essence of an existence than to speak, with
Duns Scotus, of the existence of an essence (essentia et
eius existentia).

causes it both to be and to be precisely that
which it is. He who begins to see this, however, also begins to grasp the very stuff our
universe is made of. He even begins obscurely
to perceive the supreme cause of such a world.

Why had the Greek mind spontaneously
stopped at the notion of nature, or of essence,
as at an ultimate explanation? Because, in our
human experience, existence is always that of
a particular essence. We directly know only
individual and sensible existing things whose
existence merely consists in being this and
that individual thing. The existence of an oak
tree obviously limits itself to being an oak tree
or, rather, to being this one particular oak
tree, and the same could be said of everything
else. What does this mean, if not that the essence of any and every thing is not existence
itself, but only one of the many possible shar-
ings in existence? This fact is best expressed
by the fundamental distinction of "being" and
"what is" so clearly laid down by Thomas
Aquinas. It does not mean that existence is
distinct from essence as a thing from another
thing. Once more, existence is not a thing, but
the act that causes a thing both to be and to
be what it is. This distinction merely expresses
the fact that, in our human experience, there

is no thing whose essence it is "to be," and not
"to-be-a-certain-thing." The definition of no
empirically given thing is existence; hence its
essence is not existence, but existence must be
conceived as distinct from it.

How then are we to account for the existence of a world made up of such things? You
can take them all one after the other and ask
yourself why each of them is, or exists; the
essence of no one of them will ever yield the
answer to your question. Since the nature of
no one of them is "to be," the most exhaustive
scientific knowledge of what they are will not
so much as suggest the beginning of an answer to the question: Why are they? This
world of ours is a world of change; physics,
chemistry, biology can teach us the laws according to which change actually happens in
it; what these sciences cannot teach us is why
this world, taken together with its laws, its
order, and its intelligibility, is, or exists. If
the nature of no known thing is "to be," the
nature of no known thing contains in itself the
sufficient reason for its own existence. But it
points to its sole conceivable cause. Beyond a
world wherein "to be" is everywhere at hand,
and where every nature can account for what
other natures are but not for their common

existence, there must be some cause whose very essence it is "to be." To post such a being whose essence is a pure Act of existing, that is, whose essence is not to be this and that, but "to be," is also to post the Christian God as the supreme cause of the universe. A most deeply hidden God, "He who is" is also a most obvious God. By revealing to the metaphysician that they cannot account for their own existence, all things point to the fact that there is such a supreme cause wherein essence and existence coincide. Here at last, Thomas Aquinas and Augustine ultimately meet. Because his own existential metaphysics has succeeded in forcing its way through that crust of essences which is but the outer coating of reality, Thomas Aquinas can see the pure Act of existing as one sees the presence of the cause in any one of its effects.

To reach this point was probably to reach the *ultima Thule* of the metaphysical world Saint Augustine had reached it on the strength of Christian faith, on the very day he had heard all things proclaim, in the language of the Bible: "We created not ourselves, but were created by Him who abideth for ever." To Augustine, however, "He who abideth for ever" essentially remained the self-existing "eternal Truth, true Love and loved Eter-

nity."[18] Saint Thomas Aquinas has reached it
on the strength of straight metaphysical
knowledge, where he says that "all knowing
beings implicitly know God in any and every
thing that they know."[19] It was impossible to
go further, because human reason cannot go
further than the highest of all metaphysical
principles. One might have expected at least
this, that once in possession of so fundamental
a truth, men would carefully preserve it. But
they did not. Its loss almost immediately followed its discovery. How and why it has been
lost is therefore the problem to which we now
have to turn our attention.

18. Saint Augustine, *Confessions,* Bk. X, chap. x, n. 25,
English trans., p. 227. Cf. Bk. VII, chap. x, n. 16, p. 158.
19. Saint Thomas Aquinas, *Quaestiones disputatae de
Veritate,* qu. 22, art. 2, ad 1ᵐ. Similar statements will be
found wherever Thomas Aquinas speaks about the natural and confused desire of all men for beatitude; for instance, *Summa theologica,* Pars I, qu. 2, art. 1, ad 1ᵐ.

III

GOD AND MODERN PHILOSOPHY

THE transition from medieval philosophy
to early modern philosophy is best illus-
trated by the change that took place in the social condition of the philosophers themselves.
During the Middle Ages practically all the
philosophers were monks, priests, or at least
simple clerics. From the seventeenth century
up to our own days very few churchmen have
exhibited real creative genius in the field of
philosophy. Malebranche and Condillac in
France, Berkeley in Ireland, Rosmini in Italy
can be quoted but as exceptions to the rule,
and none of them is ever reckoned among the
outstanding philosophical geniuses of modern times. Modern philosophy has been created
by laymen, not by churchmen, and to the ends
of the natural cities of men, not to the end of
the supernatural city of God.

This epoch-making change became apparent when, in the First Part of his *Discourse
upon Method*, Descartes announced his decision "to seek no other knowledge than that
which" he "was able to find within" himself

"or else in the great book of the world."[1] Descartes' statement did not mean at all that it
was his intention to do away with God, with
religion, or even with theology; but it em-
phatically meant that, in so far as he himself
was concerned, such matters were not fitting
objects for philosophical speculation. After
all, is not the way to heaven open to the most
ignorant as well as to the most learned? Does
not the Church itself teach that the revealed
truths which lead men to salvation lie beyond
the reach of our intelligence? Let religion remain to us then what it actually is in itself: a
matter of faith, not of intellectual knowledge
or of rational demonstration.

What thus happened with the philosophy
of Descartes, and quite independently from
his personal Christian conviction, was the dis-
ruption of the medieval ideal of Christian
Wisdom. To Saint Thomas Aquinas, for instance, the supreme expression of wisdom was
theology. "This sacred doctrine," Thomas
Aquinas says, "is wisdom par excellence
among all the human wisdoms; it is not highest in a certain order only, but absolutely."
And why is it so? Because the proper object

1. Descartes, *Discours de la méthode,* Première Partie,
ed. Adam-Tannery, VI, 9, ll. 21–22.

of theology is God, who is the highest conceivable object of human knowledge: "He eminently deserves to be called wise, whose consideration is about the absolutely supreme cause of the universe, that is, God."[2] As the science of the supreme cause, theology reigns supreme among all the other sciences; they all are judged by it and subordinated to it. Against this wisdom of Christian faith, Descartes was no man to raise any objection. Himself a Christian, he looked at it as at his only means of personal salvation through Christ and the Church of Christ. As a philosopher, however, he was looking for an altogether different sort of wisdom, namely, a knowledge of truth by its first causes to be attained by natural reason alone and directed toward practical temporal ends.[3] Descartes did not differ from Saint Thomas Aquinas in that he suppressed theology—he very carefully preserved it; nor in that he formally distinguished philosophy from theology—Saint Thomas Aquinas had done it many centuries

2. Saint Thomas Aquinas, *Summa theologica,* Pars I, qu. 1, art. 6, *Resp.*

3. Descartes, *Principes de la philosophie,* Préface, ed. Adam-Tannery, Part II, Vol. IX, 4, ll. 19–23. Cf. p. 5, ll. 13–18. On this point, see J. Maritain, *Le Songe de Descartes* (Paris, R.-A. Corrêa, 1932), ch. iii, "Déposition de la sagesse," pp. 79–150.

before him. What was new with Descartes
was his actual and practical separation of
philosophical wisdom and theological wisdom.
Whereas Thomas Aquinas distinguished in
order to unite, Descartes divided in order to
separate. Let the theologians take him to his
supreme supernatural Good by means of the
wisdom of faith; not only will Descartes have
no objection, but he will feel exceedingly
grateful. As he himself says: "As much as
anyone, I strive to gain heaven."[4] As a philosopher, however, Descartes was after an entirely different sort of wisdom, that is, the
rational knowledge "of the first causes and of
the true principles whence the reasons of all
that which it is possible to know can be de-
duced."[5] Such is the natural and human good,
"considered by natural reason without the
light of faith."

The immediate consequence of such an attitude should have been to bring back human
reason to the philosophical attitude of the
Greeks. Since Descartes' philosophy was
neither directly nor indirectly regulated by

4. Descartes, *Discours de la méthode*, Première Partie,
ed. Adam-Tannery, VI, 8, ll. 8-9. Exactly: "Je révérais
notre théologie, et prétendais, autant qu'aucun autre, à
gagner le ciel."

5. Descartes, *Principes de la philosophie*, Préface, p. 5,
ll. 21-24.

theology, he had no reason whatsoever to sup-
pose that their conclusions would ultimately
coincide. Why should there not have been between the object, or objects, of his religious
worship and the rational principle of intelligibility of all things the same separation there
was between his faith and his reason, or his
theology and his philosophy? It would have
been so logical for Descartes to adopt such a
position that some of his best historians do not
hesitate to maintain that in fact he did. In
O. Hamelin's own words: "Descartes comes
after the Ancients almost as though there had
been nothing else between him and them, save
only the physicists."[6]

That, logically speaking, this is what
should have happened, is beyond a doubt.
That, however, nothing of the sort did actually happen is also beyond a doubt, and the
fact is susceptible of a very simple historical
explanation. When a Greek philosopher had
to approach the problem of natural theology
by a purely rational method, he found himself
confronted only with the religious gods of
Greek mythology. Whatever his name, his
rank, or function, not one among the gods of
Greek religion had ever claimed to be the one,

6. O. Hamelin, *Le Système de Descartes* (2d ed., Paris,
Alcan, 1921), p. 15.

sole, and supreme Being, creator of the world, first principle, and ultimate end of all things. Descartes, on the contrary, could not approach the same philosophical problem without finding himself confronted with the Christian God. When a philosopher is also a Christian, he can very well say, at the beginning of his inquiry: Let me pretend that I am not a Christian; let me try to seek, by reason alone and without the light of faith, the first causes and the first principles whereby all things can be explained. As an intellectual sport, this is as good as any other one; but it is bound to result in a failure, because when a man both knows and believe that there is but one cause of all that is, the God in whom he believes can hardly be other than the cause which he knows.

The whole problem of modern natural theology is there in a nutshell, and to realize its paradoxical nature is the first condition for a correct understanding of its history. Far from coming after the Greeks as though there had been nothing in between, Descartes has come after the Greeks with the naïve condition that he could solve, by the purely rational method of the Greeks, all the problems which had been raised in between by Christian natural theology. In other words, Descartes never doubted for a single moment that the first principle of a philosophy wholly separated from Christian theology would finally prove to be the very same God whom philosophy had never been able to discover so long as it had remained foreign to the influence of Christian revelation. No wonder then that we historians do not agree on Descartes. Some of us write the history of what he said; some others write the history of what he actually did; and just as he said that he would seek truth in the light of reason alone, what he did, at least in metaphysics, was to restate the main conclusions of Christian natural theology as if Christian supernatural theology itself had never existed. To Liard, Descartes appears as the pioneer of scientific positivism; to Espinas, he appears as a faithful pupil of his first professors, the Jesuits.[7] In fact, Descartes was both, and both at one and the same time, but not with regard to the same questions.

The God of Descartes is an unmistakably Christian God. The common foundation for

7. Descartes has been interpreted by Victor Cousin as an exponent of his own spiritualistic metaphysics. Against this predominantly metaphysical interpretation of his doctrine, the scientific elements of Cartesianism have been stressed by L. Liard, *Descartes* (Paris, Alcan, 1882); later, under the influence of L. Lévy-Bruhl's unpublished lectures, by myself, in *La Liberté chez Descartes et la théologie* (Paris, Alcan, 1913). The whole problem has been reconsidered, and my own conclusions

the Cartesian demonstrations of the existence of such a God is the clear and distinct idea of a thinking, uncreated, and independent substance, which is naturally innate within the human mind. If we investigate into the cause why such an idea exists within us, we are at once led to posit, as the only conceivable explanation for it, a being who is possessed of all the attributes which attend our own idea of him, that is, a self-existing, infinite, all-powerful, one and unique being. But it is enough for us directly to consider our innate idea of him, to make sure that God is, or exists. We are so accustomed, in all other things, to make a distinction between essence and existence, that we naturally feel inclined to imagine that God can be conceived as not actually existent. Nevertheless, when we think more attentively of God, we soon find that the nonexistence of God is, strictly speaking, unthinkable. Our innate idea of God is that of a

ably corrected, by Henri Gouhier, *La Pensée religieuse de Descartes* (Paris, J. Vrin, 1924). During the same years when Lévy-Bruhl was teaching his scientific-minded Descartes, an apologetics-minded Descartes was being elaborated by A. Espinas. The result of his reflections is to be found in Espinas' posthumous book, *Descartes et la morale* (Paris, 1925), 2 vols. The latest discussion of the problem is to be found in the book of Francesco Olgiati, *Cartesio, Vita e Pensiero* (Milano, 1934).

supremely perfect being; since existence is a
perfection, to think of a supremely perfect
being to whom existence is wanting is to think
of a supremely perfect being to whom some
perfection is wanting, which is contradictory;
hence existence is inseparable from God and,
consequently, he necessarily is, or exists.[8]

It is a well-known fact that Descartes always despised history; but here history has
paid him back in full. Had he ever so little in-
vestigated into the past of his own idea of
God, he would have realized at once that
though it be true that all men have a certain
idea of the divinity, they have not all, or
always, had the Christian idea of God. If all
men had such an idea of God, Moses would
not have asked Jehovah for his name; or else
Jehovah's answer would have been: "What a
silly question! You know it." Descartes was
so anxious not to corrupt the rational purity
of his metaphysics by any admixture of Christian faith that he simply decreed the universal
innateness of the Christian definition of God.
Like the innate Ideas of Plato, Descartes' innate idea of God was a reminiscence; not
however, the reminiscence of some idea con-
templated by the soul in a former life, but

8. Descartes, *Méditations,* V, ed. Adam-Tannery, IX,
52.

simply the reminiscence of what he had learned
in church when he was a little boy.

This disconcerting indifference of Descartes toward the possible origin of so important a metaphysical idea is by no means
a unique accident in his philosophy. Of the
many things which had been said by his
predecessors, a large number appeared to him
as being at least materially true, and Descartes never hesitated to repeat them when it
suited him to do so. To him, however, to repeat something never meant to borrow it. As
Descartes himself saw it, the greatest merit of
his own philosophy consisted in this, that because it was the first one to have consistently
followed the only true method, it also was the
only one to be a continuous chain of demonstrated consequences faultlessly drawn from
evident principles. Just change, I do not say
one of the rings, but merely its place, and the
whole chain goes to pieces.[9] Where the truth
value of an idea is so wholly inseparable from
its place in the order of deduction, why should
one worry about its origin? There is but one
place where a true idea is fully true; it is the
very place it finds in Descartes' own philosophy. And the Cartesian idea of God is an

9. Descartes, *Principes de la philosophie,* Préface, IX,
19, ll. 12–26.

outstanding application of this principle. Assuredly it is the keystone of Descartes' metaphysics, but since human wisdom is one, there is no such thing as an isolated Cartesian metaphysics. What is the keystone of Cartesian metaphysics must of necessity also be the keystone of the physics which borrows its principles from metaphysics. In short, what gave to his idea of God its full value in the mind of Descartes was its remarkable aptness to become the starting point of a purely scientific interpretation of the world. Because the Cartesian God was metaphysically true, he provided science with the principles of true physics, and because no other one could provide true physics with the principles it needs for a systematic exposition, no other God but the Cartesian God could possibly be the true God.

This must be carefully kept in mind by anybody who wishes to understand the curious metaphysical adventures of Descartes' God. By origin, he was the Christian God. Not only was he a Being as wholly self-subsisting as the God of Saint Thomas Aquinas himself, but Descartes would gladly have made him even more so, if the thing had been possible at all. His own God was not simply a pure Act of existing which had no cause for his own exist-

ence; he was like an infinite energy of self-
existence which, so to speak, was to itself the
cause of its own existence. Of course, there are
no words to describe such a God. Since a cause
naturally appears to us as distinct from its
effect, it is awkward to speak of him as if he
were his own cause. Yet, could we bring the
two notions of cause and effect to coincide, at
least in this unique case, an infinitely powerful self-causing Being would perhaps be the
least inadequate of all the human approxima-
tions of God.[10]

At first sight, the God of Descartes and the
God of Saint Thomas Aquinas do not seem to
differ by more than a shade of metaphysical
thought. But there is more in this than meets
the eye. When Thomas Aquinas had trans-
figured the supreme Thought of Aristotle
into the Christian "He who is," he had raised
a first philosophical principle up to the level
of God. Starting from this very same Christian God, Descartes was now using him as a
first philosophical principle. True enough, the
God in whom, as a Christian, Descartes believed was the selfsame God whom, as a phi-

10. For a detailed discussion of this notion of God and
of the texts of Descartes where it is formulated, see É.
Gilson, *Études sur le rôle de la pensée médiévale dans la
formation du système cartésien* (Paris, J. Vrin, 1930).

losopher, he knew to be the supreme cause of all things; the fact however remains that, as a philosopher, Descartes had no use for God taken in himself and in his absolute self-sufficient perfection. To him God in himself was an object of religious faith; what was an object of rational knowledge was God taken as the highest among the "Principles of Philosophy." This is the reason why the natural theology of Descartes not only limited itself to the consideration of those among the divine attributes that account for the existence of the world but also conceived these attributes as they have to be conceived in order to account for the existence of a Cartesian world.

What the Cartesian world of science was everybody knows. It is an exclusively mechanical universe, wherein everything can be accounted for by the geometrical properties of space and the physical laws of motion.[11] If we look at God as the only possible explanation for the existence of such a world, his main attribute must necessarily be not the self-contemplation of his own infinite Being, but his self-causing all-powerfulness, source of his creative causality. Instead of the self-suffi-

11. Descartes, *op. cit.,* Deuxième Partie, IX, chap. lxiv, 101–102.

cient and self-knowing Being of Thomas Aquinas, we now have a self-causing energy of existence. Were we to resort to metaphors, we might say that whereas the God of Saint Thomas was an infinite ocean of existence, the God of Descartes is an infinitely powerful fountain of existence. And it is not difficult to see why. Since the ultimate philosophical function of his God was to be a cause, the Cartesian God had to be possessed of any and every attribute which was required of the creator of a Cartesian world. Such a world being indefinitely extended in space, its creator had to be infinite; such a world being purely mechanical and devoid of final causes, what was true and good in it had to be such because God had created it by a free decree of his will, and not conversely; the mechanical world of Descartes rested upon the assumption of the conservation of the same quantity of motion in the universe; hence the God of Descartes had to be an immutable God and the laws established by his will could not be allowed to change, unless this world itself be first destroyed. In short, the essence of the Cartesian God was largely determined by his philosophical function, which was to create and to preserve the mechanical world of

science as Descartes himself conceived it.[12]
Now it is quite true that a Creator is an eminently Christian God, but a God whose very
essence is to be a creator is not a Christian
God at all. The essence of the true Christian
God is not to create but to be. "He who is" can
also create, if he chooses; but he does not
exist because he creates, nay, not even himself; he can create because he supremely is.

We are now beginning to see why, and in
what sense, the metaphysics of Descartes was
a decisive moment in the evolution of natural
theology. Evolution, however, is not always
synonymous with progress; and this time it
was destined to be a regress. I am not arguing

12. Hence the justly famous remark of Pascal: "I
cannot forgive Descartes. In all his philosophy he would
have been quite willing to dispense with God. But he had
to make Him give a fillip to set the world in motion;
beyond this, he had no further need of God." *Pascal's
Pensées,* trans. W. F. Trotter, pp. 153–154, Everyman's
Library. This physicism, or naturalism, which pervades
the natural theology of Descartes, has been keenly observed and admirably analyzed by Maurice Blondel,
"L'Anti-cartésianisme de Malebranche," in *Revue de
métaphysique et de morale,* 1916, pp. 1–26. The only addi-
tion I would like to make to this most excellent essay is
that Malebranche has tried to express his own anticarte-
sian spirit in terms of Cartesian philosophy. Hence his
personal difficulties. In his effort to re-Christianize the
natural theology of Descartes, Malebranche has Cartesianized the Christian God.

here on the dogmatic assumption that the God
of Saint Thomas is the true God. What I am
trying to make clear is the objective fact that,
even as a philosophical supreme cause, the
God of Descartes was a stillborn God. He
could not possibly live because, as Descartes
had conceived him, he was the God of Christianity reduced to the condition of philosophical principle, in short, an infelicitous hybrid
of religious faith and of rational thought. The
most striking characteristic of such a God was
that his creative function had integrally absorbed his essence. Hence, the name that was
hereafter going to be his truest name: no
longer "He who is" but rather "The Author of
Nature." Assuredly, the God of Christianity
had always been the Author of Nature, but he
had always been infinitely more than that,
whereas, after Descartes, he was destined progressively to become nothing else than that.
Descartes himself was too good a Christian to
consider Nature as a particular god; but,
strangely enough, it never occurred to him
that to reduce the Christian God himself to no
more than the supreme cause of Nature was to
do identically the same thing. Metaphysical
conclusions so necessarily follow from their
principles that Descartes himself reached at

once what were to be the ultimate conclusions
of his eighteenth-century disciples when he
wrote the following sentence: "By Nature,
considered in general, I am now understanding nothing else than either God, or the order
and the disposition established by God in
created things."[13]

The most immediate historical effect of this
Cartesian natural theology has been again to
dissociate God as an object of religious worship from God as a first principle of philosophical intelligibility. Hence the famous pro-
test of Pascal: "The God of Christians is not
a God who is simply the author of mathematical truths, or of the order of the elements;
that is the view of heathens and Epicureans
. . . ; but the God of Abraham, the God of
Isaac, the God of Jacob, the God of Christians, is a God of love and of comfort, a God
who fills the soul and heart of those whom he
possesses."[14] In a sense it can be said that the
greatest among the immediate successors of
Descartes did all that was humanly conceivable to restore the unity of natural theology
on the basis of Cartesian principles. If they

13. Descartes, *Méditations,* VI, ed. Adam-Tannery, IX,
64.
14. *Pascal's Pensées,* pp. 153–154.

failed, as I am afraid they did, the reason for
their failure probably was that such an undertaking was in itself a contradictory one and,
consequently, that the thing could not be done
at all.

Had it been possible successfully to achieve
such a task, Malebranche would have been the
most likely man to do it. Himself a priest of
the Oratory, a deeply pious man, almost a
mystic, Malebranche combined in his own person all the conditions required in order to succeed in this philosophical experiment. As a
physicist, he felt perfectly satisfied with the
mechanical principles laid down by Descartes;
as a metaphysician, he had worked out an
original synthesis of Cartesianism and Augus-
tinianism which posited God as the sole source
of causal efficacy both in the order of human
knowledge and in the order of physical causality; as a theologian, he would maintain that
God always acts in conformity with that which
He is and that the only end of God in His ac-
tion is His own glory in the person of Jesus
Christ. What is God, Malebranche asks, if not
Being itself? "I think I understand you correctly," Ariste says in one of Malebranche's
dialogues, "you are defining God just as,
speaking to Moses, He has defined Himself:

God is the One who Is."[15] Is not this, one may ask, the truly and genuinely Christian God?

It no doubt is. An infinitely perfect Being, the God of Malebranche "is to Himself His own light, He discovers in His own substance the essences of all beings and all their possible modalities, and, in His decrees, their existence as well as all their actual modalities."[16] There is not a single word in this definition that would not apply just as well to the God of Saint Thomas Aquinas. Far from conceding to Descartes that God freely creates eternal truths, Malebranche restores in full the Augustinian doctrine of a God who knows all things, both actual and possible, by knowing his own eternal Ideas, and who knows his Ideas by knowing his own substance. Here, however, is the loose joint, where the Cartesian spirit has leaked into the natural theology of Malebranche. In a way, a God who sees nothing but in his own substance, and who there sees all beings together with all

15. Malebranche, *Entretiens sur la métaphysique et sur la religion,* ed. Paul Fontana (A. Colin, 1922), Vol. I, chap. ii, sec. 4, p. 46. For a general exposition of Malebranche's doctrine, see Henri Gouhier, *La Vocation de Malebranche* (Paris, J. Vrin, 1926), and *La Philosophie de Malebranche et son expérience religieuse* (Paris, J. Vrin, 1926).

16. Malebranche, *Entretiens sur la métaphysique et sur la religion,* Vol. I, chap. viii, sec. 10, p. 182.

their intelligible relations, is the very reverse
of the God of Descartes. But, curiously
enough, the difference between these two Gods
is due to the fact that Malebranche has
thoroughly Cartesianized the, to him, insuffi-
ciently Cartesian God of Descartes. The
world of Descartes had been a world of intelligible laws established by the arbitrary will
of an all-powerful God; Malebranche's origi-
nality was to conceive God himself as an infinite world of intelligible laws. Nothing more
closely resembles the supreme Intellect of Plotinos than the divine Word of Malebranche.
Many historians would say they are the same.
At any rate, they are so much alike that one
might almost define the Word of Malebranche
as a Plotinian Intellect which has turned Cartesian. In short, with Malebranche, the Creator himself has to submit to the very type of
intelligibility which the God of Descartes had
freely imposed upon created things.

The net result of Malebranche's metaphysical venture has been the rise of a supernatural
God whose inner life was conceived after the
pattern of a Cartesian world. By simply
knowing in himself all his possible finite par-
ticipations, the God of Malebranche knows
all conceivable beings and all their conceivable
relations. He knows all their quantitative re-

lations as comprised within his single and
simple idea of the intelligible extension. In
other words, the physics of God is the same as
that of Descartes. And how could it be otherwise? Since the only true world is the geometrical world of Descartes, where everything
can be accounted for by the sole properties of
extension in space, God himself can know and
create matter but through the intelligible idea
of extension. Since all speculative truths
bear upon relations of extension, the world of
matter is known by God, just as Descartes
himself thought he knew it, through this
simple knowledge of all the possible relations
of extension.

How then are we to account for the fact
that, among the infinite number of possible
systems of relations in space, God singled out
precisely the one we live in, in order to create
it? Malebranche's answer to this question is
that, besides the relations of quantity, there
are relations of perfection. Two and two make
four is a relation in the order of quantity;
man is superior to beasts is a relation in the
order of perfection. Now, just as quantitative
relations are purely speculative in kind, relations of perfection are practical by definition.
What appears to us as better is that which
appears to us as more lovable. So is it with

God. Taken together, all the possible relations of perfection between all the possible
beings form an infinite system, which we call
Order. Now "God invincibly loves this immutable Order, which consists, and can consist, but in the relations of perfection there
are between his own attributes, as well as between the ideas that are comprised within his
own substance." God then could not love, or
will, anything that contradicts this eternal
and absolute Order without loving and willing
against his own perfection, which is impossible.[17] This is why God has created this one
world such as it is. It is not, absolutely speaking, the most perfect possible world, but it is
at least the most perfect world which God
could possibly create, given that it had to be a
world ruled by universal, uniform, and intelligible laws.[18] A congeries of individually
perfect things would not be a whole, nor would
it be a world, because it would not be an order
of things regulated by laws.

Perhaps the best way for us to understand
the God of Malebranche is to ask ourselves
this question: Granting that the Cartesian
world is the most intelligible of all possible
worlds, why has God singled out just that one

17. *Ibid.*, Vol. I, chap. viii, sec. 13, pp. 185–187.
18. *Ibid.*, Vol. II, chap. ix, sec. 10, pp. 209–211.

in order to create it? To which the answer
naturally is because God is supremely intelligent, he could not fail to do what Descartes
would have done, had Descartes been God.
Strikingly enough, this is exactly how Descartes himself had asked the question at the
beginning of his unfinished treatise on "The
World"; not at all: What is this universe
made of? but rather: Supposing we had to
create out of nothing a perfectly rational universe, how would we go at it? Malebranche did
nothing more than to go one step further
along the same road. To the question: Could
God have created another universe? the answer of Saint Thomas had been: Yes, certainly; since God is perfect, the world which
he has created is very good, but he could have
created many different good ones, and why,
among these many possible universes, he has
singled out this one to grant it existence, we
don't know: He is free. Malebranche, too, had
always maintained that God was eternally
free to create or not to create; but he added
that, since God had freely chosen to create,
his own perfection bound him to create the
best world is was possible for a God acting as
becomes a perfect God to create.

Clearly enough, the notion of perfection is
here taking precedence over the notion of be-

ing. Malebranche still calls God, Being; in
fart, however, and under the dominant influence of Augustine, he conceives him like the
Good of Plotinos and of Plato. Now, even the
Good is as essence, or nature, and there is a
vast difference between saying that God cannot not exist because he is perfect, and saying
that God cannot not be perfect because he is
"He who is." Malebranche says the second
but he thinks the first. Consequently, this
most pious disciple of Saint Augustine uncon-
sciously goes back to the awkward position
which had been that of his master thirteen
centuries before him: he has not the natural
philosophy of his revealed theology; the God
of his philosophy is not the same as the God
of his religion.

There is nothing surprising in such a fact.
In so far as his philosophical method was concerned, Malebranche was a Cartesian. One of
the deepest exigencies, and probably the deepest exigency, of the Cartesian method is never
to go from things to ideas, but on the contrary
from ideas to things. Existences are given to
a Cartesian only through, and in, essences.
God himself could not be posited as actually
existing were it not for the fact that his idea
is in us, and that, as it is found there, it involves existence. As the Decartes of the fifth

Meditation explicitly says: since we cannot
possibly separate existence from the idea of
God, God necessarily is, or exists. Despite the
shades of thought that are proper to his own
system, Malebranche's position has remained
substantially the same: "One cannot see the essence of the Infinite without its existence, the
idea of Being without being."[19] Such also, and
for the same reason, was the position of Leibniz, whose favorite proof of the existence of
God posits him as the only conceivable cause
of the essences, and therefore as the necessary
Being whose essence includes existence, "or in
whom possibility is sufficient to produce actuality." One could hardly wish for a more perfect formula of the primacy of essence over
existence: "God alone, or the Necessary Being, has this prerogative, that if he be possible [that is: if his essence be conceivable
without contradiction] he must necessarily
exist."[20]

If one keeps in mind that God is that Being
whose very possibility produces his actuality,
he will not feel surprised to learn that the
world created by such a God is also the only

19. *Ibid.,* Vol. I, chap. ii, sec. 5, p. 47.
20. Leibniz, *Monadology,* nn. 44, 45; English trans. by
G. R. Montgomery, in *Discourse on Metaphysics, Corre-
spondence with Arnauld and Monadology* (2d ed., The
Open Court Co., 1918), p. 258.

one which such a God could possibly have
created. The best definition of the Leibnizian
God is an absolutely perfect being.[21] As such,
the God of Leibniz is also to be an infinitely
generous God; and because, morally speaking
at least, he can hardly refrain from communi-
cating his own perfection, he has to create.
Now a perfect God can create only the best
possible world. Among the infinite series of
possible worlds, the best one obviously will be
the one wherein the highest conceivable rich-
ness of effects will be achieved by the simplest
possible means. As Leibniz himself says, this
is what the mathematicians call a problem of
maximum and *minimum*. Such problems are
susceptible of but one solution. Consequently,
the best possible world is exactly the one we
are in.[22] A most gratifying certitude indeed,
at least so long as it lasts, and Voltaire was to
see to it that it did not outlive the earthquake
of Lisbon. The metaphysical difficulty however was not there; it rather lay in the fact
that Leibniz pretended to make us accept as
the supreme Being a God who was but a nature. As a matter of fact, the God of the
Monadology was but the Good of Plato, solv-
ing the problem of which world to create, by

21. Leibniz, *Discourse on Metaphysics,* chap. i, p. 3.
22. *Ibid.,* chap. v, pp. 8–9.

means of the infinitesimal calculus recently discovered by Leibniz.

The greatest metaphysician among the successors of Descartes was Spinoza, because, with him, somebody at last said about God what Descartes himself, if not as a Christian, at least as a philosopher, should have thought and said from the very beginning. Descartes had been either religiously right and philosophically wrong, or philosophically right and religiously wrong; Spinoza has been wholly right or wholly wrong, either philosophically or religiously. Spinoza had neither the religion of a Christian nor that of a Jew; having no religion whatsoever, he could not be expected to have the philosophy of any religion; but he was a thoroughbred philosopher, which accounts for the fact that he at least has had the religion of his philosophy. His God is an absolutely infinite being, or substance, which is "cause of itself" because its "essence involves existence."[23] The primacy of essence is here so forcefully stressed that nobody can miss its metaphysical significance. In the doctrine of Descartes, one may still

23. *Spinoza's Ethics,* Part I, definitions 1 and 6, English trans., p. 1, Everyman's Library. On Spinoza's philosophy, see Victor Delbos, *Le Spinozisme* (Paris, Société Française d'Imprimerie et de Librairie, 1916).

wonder if God's essence involves his existence
in himself, or in our own mind only; in the
Ethics of Spinoza, no hesitation remains
possible. Just as a square circle cannot exist
because its essence is a contradictory one, God
cannot not exist because, in Spinoza's own
words, "the existence of substance *follows
from its nature alone*, for that involves existence."[24] Let us therefore conceive a universe
wherein the existence of any and every thing
expresses but the power to exist which belongs
to its nature; only one being can be there
posited as necessarily existing; it is God, or
the being absolutely infinite, which, because
it "has an infinite power of existence from itself," absolutely is, or exists.[25] But a God who
"exists and acts merely from the necessity of
his nature,"[26] is nothing more than a nature.
Rather he is nature itself: *Deus sive Natura*.[27]
God is the absolute essence whose intrinsic
necessity makes necessary the being of all that
is, so that he is absolutely all that is, just as,
in as much as it is, all that it is "necessarily involves the eternal and infinite essence of
God."[28]

24. *Spinoza's Ethics,* Part I, prop. 11, p. 8.
25. *Ibid.,* p. 9.
26. *Ibid.,* Part I, Appendix, p. 30.
27. *Ibid.,* Part IV, Preface, p. 142.
28. *Ibid.,* Part II, prop. 45, p. 72.

Spinoza has often been branded as an atheist by his adversaries; he has also been called, by one of his German admirers, "a man inebriated with God."[29] What renders Spinoza so important in the history of natural theology is that both judgments are true. A religious atheist, Spinoza was truly inebriated with his philosophical God.[30] Positive religions as he saw them were but anthropomorphic superstitions invented by men for practical and political purposes. It is no wonder that, to Jews as well as to Christians, he always appeared as a godless man. But we must not forget the other side of the picture. As a philosopher, and toward his own philosophical God, Spinoza probably is the most pious thinker there ever was. Marcus Aurelius and Plato could perhaps compete with him for the title; but Plato had never gone so far as to worship the Good, and as for Marcus Aurelius' religion, it had never been more than his acceptance of an order of things which he could not change. Spinoza could do much more than accept nature; by thoroughly under-

29. Novalis.

30. On Spinoza's criticism of positive religions, see his *Theologico-Political Treatise,* and, before anything else, the unambiguous and outspoken statement of his position in his *Ethics,* Part I, Appendix, pp. 30–36.

standing it as an absolutely intelligible reality, he was progressively liberating himself
from illusion, error, evil, mental slavery, and
achieving that supreme human beatitude
which is inseparable from spiritual liberty. I,
personally, would not speak lightly of Spinoza's religion. It is a one hundred per cent
metaphysically pure answer to the question
how to achieve human salvation by means of
philosophy only. I am well aware of the fact
that what I myself hold as the true religion,
that is, Christianity, appeared to him but a
piece of childish mythology. But I feel infinitely grateful to him because, after having
discarded all positive religion as purely mytho-
logical, he did not replace it by a philosophical
mythology of his own. Spinoza is a Jew who
turned "Him who is" into a mere "that which
is"; and he could love "that which is," but he
never expected that he himself would be loved
by it. The only way for us to overcome Spinoza is, in a truly Spinozistic way, to free
ourselves from his limitation by understanding it as a limitation. This means, to grasp
again Being as the existence of essence, not as
the essence of existence; to touch it as an act,
not to conceive it as a thing. Spinoza's metaphysical experiment is the conclusive demon-

stration of at least this: That any religious
God whose true name is not "He who is" is
nothing but a myth.

One of the most delectable objects of contemplation for the connoisseurs of human silli-
ness is precisely the myth which seems to have
haunted so many minds from the middle of the
seventeenth century up to the end of the eighteenth. "Haunted" is here the correct word,
for this curious myth was but the philosophical ghost of the Christian God. The Deists,
whose history has been several times ably
sketched but never written in full, have always been considered by Christians as being
at bottom simple atheists. "Deism," Bossuet
says, "that is, Atheism in disguise."[31] A somewhat oversimplified statement of the case but
nevertheless a true one, at least in so far as the
God of any positive religion was concerned.
The Deists were in full agreement with Spinoza on the fabulous character of any so-
called revealed God. On the other side, and
their very name shows it, they themselves had
a God, but though they were most emphatic
on the fact that he was a naturally known
God, they did not at all conceive him as the
philosophers had done. The God of the Deists

31. J. B. Bossuet, *The History of the Variations of the
Protestant Churches*, Bk. V, chap. xxxi.

was not a first intelligible principle like the
Good of Plato, the self-thinking Thought of
Aristotle, or the Infinite Substance of Spinoza. The God of the Deists, as Dryden describes him in his famous Epistle, *Religio
Laici; or, a Layman's Fate*, was a supreme
Being, universally worshiped by all men in the
same way, by the sole rules of Praise and
Pray; yet a God Who could be offended by
crime, and Who, when men sinned, expected
them to atone for their faults by repentance;
last, not least, their God was a God Whose
justice had ultimately to be satisfied, if not in
this life, then in another, where the good will
reap reward, the bad punishment.[32]

Dryden himself was not a Deist, but his description of their doctrine was correct; and
what was their doctrine if not this curious

32. Deism is at least as old as the sixteenth century. In
his *Instruction Chrétienne* (1563), the Calvinist divine
Viret criticizes people who believe in God but not in
Christ, and according to whom the teachings of the Gos-
pels are just so many fables. On English Deism, see the
article "Christianisme rationnel," in *Dictionnaire de
théologie catholique*, Vol. II, col. 2415–2417. A good introduction to the problem of Deism in general is the
article "Déisme," in the same dictionary, Vol. IV, col.
232–243; bibliography, col. 243. For a more scholarly discussion of the problem, see Max Frischeisen-Köhler and
Willy Moog, *Die Philosophie der Neuzeit bis zum Ende
des XVIII. Jahrhunderts* (Berlin, 1924), pp. 376–380;
bibliography, pp. 688–689.

sample of mental teratology, a natural Christianity? The very title of the famous book published in 1696 by John Toland contained the whole of Deism in a nutshell; I was about to say that title should have become the Deist's slogan: *Christianity Not Mysterious*. Toland's book was burned by the hangman at Dublin in 1697, but the natural theology of Deism, just as it had preceded the publication of the book, survived its condemnation. Represented in England by many writers, Herbert of Cherbury (1581–1648), Charles Blount (1654–1693), and Matthew Tindal (1653–1733), it dominated the French eighteenth century with men as widely different as Voltaire and Rousseau, until the cult of the Supreme Being was officially established by Robespierre at the time of the French Revolution.

I know of no greater tribute ever paid to the God of Christianity than His survival in this idea, maintained against Christianity itself and on the strength of pure natural reason. For almost two centuries—for I myself could quote French Deists whom I have personally known—this ghost of the Christian God has been attended by the ghost of Christian religion: a vague feeling of religiosity, a

sort of trusting familiarity with some supremely good fellow to whom other good fel-
lows can hopefully apply when they are in
trouble: *le Dieu des bonnes gens.* As an object
of religious worship, however, the God of the
Deists was but the wraith of the living God of
Abraham, of Isaac, and of Jacob. As an object of pure philosophical speculation, he was
little more than a myth whose death sentence
had been irrevocably passed by Spinoza.
Having forgotten, together with "Him who
is," the true meaning of the problem of existence, Fontenelle, Voltaire, Rousseau, and so
many others with them had naturally to fall
back upon the most superficial interpretation
of the problem of final causes. God then became the "watchmaker" of Fontenelle and of
Voltaire, the supreme engineer of the huge
machine which this world is. In short, God
became again what he had already been in the
Timaeus of Plato: a Demiurge, the only difference being that this time, before beginning
to arrange his world, the Demiurge had con-
sulted Newton. Just like the Demiurge of
Plato, the God of the Deists was but a philosophical myth. Strangely enough, what our
own contemporaries are still asking themselves is whether this myth actually exists or

not? Their answer is that it does not. And our contemporaries are right in giving the question such an answer; but the fact that there is no Demiurge does not prove that there is no God.

IV

GOD AND CONTEMPORARY
THOUGHT

THE present-day position of the problem of God is wholly dominated by the
thought of Immanuel Kant and of Auguste
Comte. Their doctrines are about as widely
different as two philosophical doctrines can
possibly be. Yet the Criticism of Kant and the
Positivism of Comte have this in common, that
in both doctrines the notion of knowledge is
reduced to that of scientific knowledge, and
the notion of scientific knowledge itself to the
type of intelligibility provided by the physics
of Newton. The verb "to know" then means to
express observable relations between given
facts in terms of mathematical relations.[1] Now,
however we look at it, no given fact answers to
our notion of God. Since God is not an object
of empirical knowledge, we have no concept of
him. Consequently God is no object of knowledge, and what we call natural theology is just
idle talking.

1. For a general introduction to the criticism of meta-
physics by Kant and Comte, see É. Gilson, *The Unity of
Philosophical Experience* (New York, Scribner, 1937),
Part III, pp. 223–295.

If we compare it with the Kantian revolution, the Cartesian revolution hardly deserved
such a name. From Thomas Aquinas to Descartes the distance is assuredly a long one.
Yet, although extremely far from each other,
they are on comparable lines of thought. Between Kant and them, the line has been broken.
Coming after the Greeks, the Christian philosophers had asked themselves the question:
How obtain from Greek metaphysics an answer to the problems raised by the Christian
God? After centuries of patient work, one of
them had at last found the answer, and that is
why we find Thomas Aquinas constantly using the language of Aristotle in order to
say Christian things. Coming after the Christian philosophers, Descartes, Leibniz, Malebranche, and Spinoza found themselves confronted with this new problem: How find a
metaphysical justification for the world of
seventeenth-century science? As scientists,
Descartes and Leibniz had no metaphysics of
their own. Just as Augustine and Thomas
Aquinas had had to borrow their technique
from the Greeks, Descartes and Leibniz had
to borrow their technique from the Christian
philosophers who had preceded them. Hence
the vast number of scholastic expressions which
we meet in the works of Descartes, Leibniz,

Spinoza, and even Locke. All of them freely use the language of the Schoolmen in order to express nonscholastic views of a nonscholastic world. Yet all of them appear to us as seeking in a more or less traditional metaphysics the ultimate justification of the mechanical world of modern science. In short, and this is true of Newton himself, the supreme principle of the intelligibility of nature remains, for all of them, the Author of Nature, that is, God.[2]

With the Criticism of Kant and the Positivism of Comte, things become entirely different. Since God is not an object apprehended in the a priori forms of sensibility, space and time, he cannot be related to anything else by the category of causality. Hence, Kant concludes, God may well be a pure idea of reason, that is, a general principle of unification of our cognitions; he is not an object of cognition. Or we may have to posit his existence as required by the exigencies of practical reason; the existence of God then becomes a postulate, it is still not a cognition. In his own way, which was a much more radical one, Comte at once reached identically the same conclusion. Science,

2. For a contemporary discussion of the scientific notion of cause, see Émile Meyerson, *Identité et réalité* (2d ed., Paris, Alcan, 1912), p. 42. *De l'explication dans les sciences* (Paris, Alcan, 1921), I, 57; *Essais* (Paris, J. Vrin, 1936), pp. 28–58.

Comte says, has no use for the notion of cause. Scientists never ask themselves *why* things happen, but *how* they happen. Now as soon as you substitute the positivist's notion of relation for the metaphysical notion of cause, you at once lose all right to wonder *why* things are, and why they are what they are. To dismiss all such questions as irrelevant to the order of positive knowledge is, at the same time, to cut the very root of all speculation concerning the nature and existence of God.

It had taken Christian thinkers thirteen centuries to achieve a perfectly consistent philosophy of the universe of Christianity. It has taken modern scientists about two centuries to achieve a perfectly consistent philosophy of the mechanical universe of modern science. This is a fact which it is very important for us to realize, because it clearly shows where the pure philosophical positions are actually to be found.

If what we are after is a rational interpretation of the world of science given as an ultimate fact, either the Criticism of Kant himself or some edition of his Criticism revised to suit the demands of today's science should provide us with a satisfactory answer to our question. We might nevertheless prefer the Positivism of Comte, or some revised edition

of it. A large number among our own contemporaries actually subscribe to one or the
other of these two possible attitudes. The Neo-
Criticism has been represented by such men
as Paulsen and Vaihinger in Germany, by
Renouvier in France; and it has found what
will perhaps remain its purest formulation in
the works of our own contemporary, Professor Leon Brunschvicg. As to Positivism, it
has found important supporters in England,
John Stuart Mill and Herbert Spencer, for
instance; in France, Émile Littré, Émile Durk-
heim, and the whole French sociological
school; and it has recently been revived, under
a new form, by the Neo-Positivism of the
Vienna school. Whatever their many differences, all these schools have at least this in
common, that their ambition does not extend
beyond achieving a rational interpretation of
the world of science given as an irreducible
and ultimate fact.

But if we do not think that science is adequate to rational knowledge,[3] if we hold that
other than scientifically answerable problems

3. A critical discussion of this unduly restricted notion
of rational knowledge is to be found in J. Maritain, *The
Degrees of Knowledge* (New York, Scribner, 1938); and
also in W. R. Thompson, F.R.S., *Science and Common
Sense, an Aristotelian Excursion* (New York, Longmans,
Green, 1937), pp. 47–50.

can still be rationally posed concerning the universe, then there is no use for us to stop at the eighteenth-century Author of Nature. Why should we content ourselves with the ghost of God when we can have God? But there is no reason either why we should waste our time in weighing the respective merits of the gods of Spinoza, of Leibniz, or of Descartes. We now know what these gods are: mere by-products born of the philosophical decomposition of the Christian living God. Today our only choice is not Kant or Descartes; it is rather Kant or Thomas Aquinas. All the other positions are but halfway houses on the roads which lead either to absolute religious agnosticism or to the natural theology of Christian metaphysics.[4]

Philosophical halfway houses have always been pretty crowded, but never more than they are in our own times, especially in the field of natural theology. This fact is not a wholly inexplicable one. What makes it difficult for us to go back to Thomas Aquinas is Kant. Modern men are held spellbound by science, in some cases because they know it, but in an incomparably larger number of cases because

4. Cf. the philosophical manifesto of Rudolf Eucken, *Thomas von Aquino und Kant, ein Kampf zweier Welten* (Berlin, Reuther and Richard, 1901).

they know that, to those who know science, the
problem of God does not appear susceptible
of a scientific formulation. But what makes it
difficult for us to go as far as Kant is, if not
Thomas Aquinas himself, at least the whole
order of facts which provides a basis for his
own natural theology. Quite apart from any
philosophical demonstration of the existence
of God, there is such a thing as a spontaneous
natural theology. A quasi-instinctive tendency, observable in most men, seems to invite
them to wonder from time to time if, after all,
there is not such an unseen being as the one we
call God. The current objection that such a
feeling is but a survival in us of primitive
myths, or of our own early religious education, is not a very strong one. Primitive myths
do not account for the human belief in the
existence of the Divinity; obviously, it is the
reverse which is true. Early religious education is no sufficient explanation for the questions which sometimes arise in the minds of
men concerning the reality or unreality of
God. Some among us have received a decidedly
antireligious education; others have had no
religious education at all; and there are even
quite a few who, having once received a religious education, fail to find in its memory any

incentive to think too seriously of God.[5] The natural invitations to apply his mind to the problem come to man from quite different sources. These are the very selfsame sources which once gave rise not only to Greek mythology but to all mythologies. God spontaneously offers himself to most of us, more as a confusedly felt presence than as an answer to any problem, when we find ourselves confronted with the vastness of the ocean, the still purity of mountains, or the mysterious life of a midsummer starry sky. Far from being social in essence, these fleeting temptations to think of God usually visit us in our moments of solitude. But there is no more solitary solitude than that of a man in deep sorrow or confronted with the tragic perspective of his own impending end. "One dies alone," Pascal says. That is perhaps the reason why so many men finally meet God waiting for them on the threshold of death.

What do such feelings prove? Absolutely nothing. They are not proofs but facts, the very facts which give philosophers occasion to ask themselves precise questions concerning the possible existence of God. Just as such

5. Knowing the temptations to which historians sometimes succumb, I deem it safer to specify that there is nothing autobiographical in this last remark.

personal experiences precede any attempt to prove that there is a God, they survive our failures to prove it. Pascal did not make much of the so-called proofs of God's existence. To him, it was incomprehensible that God should exist, and it was incomprehensible that God should not exist; then he would simply wager that God exist—a safe betting indeed, since there was much to gain and nothing to lose. Thus to bet is not to know, especially in a case when, if we lose, we cannot even hope to know it. Yet Pascal was still willing to bet on what he could not know. Similarly, after proving in his *Critique of Pure Reason* that the existence of God could not be demonstrated, Kant still insisted on keeping God as at least a unifying idea in the order of speculative reason and as postulate in the moral order of practical reason. It may even appear to be true that, out of its own nature, the human mind is equally unable both to prove the existence of any God and "to escape its deep-seated instinct to personify its intellectual conceptions."[6] Whether we make it the result of spontaneous judgment of reason, with Thomas

6. Thomas Henry Huxley, *The Evolution of Theology: an Anthropological Study,* as quoted in Julian Huxley, *Essays in Popular Science* (London, Pelican Books, 1937), p. 123.

Aquinas; or an innate idea, with Descartes; or
an intellectual intuition, with Malebranche;
or an idea born of the unifying power of human reason, with Kant; or a phantasm of
human imagination, with Thomas Henry
Huxley, this common notion of God is there as
a practically universal fact whose speculative
value may well be disputed, but whose existence cannot be denied. The only problem is
for us to determine the truth value of this
notion.

At first sight, the shortest way to test it
seems to judge it from the point of view of
scientific knowledge. But the shortest way
might not be the safest one. This method rests
upon the assumption that nothing can be rationally known unless it be scientifically
known, which is far from being an evident
proposition. The names of Kant and of Comte
have very little importance, if any, in the history of modern science; Descartes and Leibniz, two of the creators of modern science, have
also been great metaphysicians. The simple
truth may be that while human reason remains one and the same in dealing with different orders of problems, it nevertheless must
approach these various orders of problems in
as many different ways. Whatever our final
answer to the problem of God may be, we all

agree that God is not an empirically observable fact. Mystical experience itself is
both unspeakable and intransmissible; hence,
it cannot become an objective experience. If,
speaking in the order of pure natural knowledge, the proposition "God exists" makes any
sense at all, it must be for its rational value
as a philosophical answer to a metaphysical
question.

When a man falls to wondering whether
there is such a being as God, he is not conscious of raising a scientific problem, or hop-
ing to give it a scientific solution. Scientific
problems are all related to the knowledge of
what given things actually are. An ideal
scientific explanation of the world would be an
exhaustive rational explanation of *what* the
world actually is; but *why* nature exists is not
a scientific problem, because its answer is not
susceptible of empirical verification. The notion of God, on the contrary, always appears
to us in history as an answer to some existential problem, that is, as the *why* of a certain
existence. The Greek gods were constantly
invoked in order to account for various "hap-
penings" in the history of men as well as in
that of things. A religious interpretation of
nature never worries about what things are—
that is a problem for scientists—but it is very

much concerned with the questions why things happen to be precisely what they are, and why they happen to be at all. The Jewish-Christian God to whom we are introduced by the Bible is there at once posited as the ultimate explanation for the very existence of man, for the present condition of man upon earth, for all the successive events that make up the history of the Jewish people as well as for these momentous events: the Incarnation of Christ and the Redemption of man by Grace. Whatever their ultimate value, these are existential answers to existential questions. As such, they cannot possibly be transposed into terms of science, but only into terms of an existential metaphysics. Hence these two immediate consequences: that natural theology is in bondage not to the method of positive science but to the method of metaphysics, and that it can correctly ask its own problems only in the frame of an existential metaphysics.

Of these two conclusions, the first one is doomed to remain very unpopular. To tell the whole truth, it sounds perfectly absurd to say, and ridiculous to maintain, that the highest metaphysical problems in no way depend upon the answers given by science to its own questions. The most common view of this matter is best expressed by these words of a

modern astronomer: "Before the philosophers
have a right to speak, science ought first to be
asked to tell all she can as to ascertain facts
and provisional hypotheses. Then, and then
only, may discussion legitimately pass into
the realms of philosophy."[7] This, I quite
agree, looks much more sensible than what I
myself have said. But when people behave as
if what I have said were false, what does happen? In 1696, John Toland decided to discuss
religious problems by a method borrowed
from natural philosophy. The result was his
book, which I have already mentioned: *Christianity Not Mysterious*. Now, if Christianity

7. Sir James Jeans, *The Mysterious Universe* (London,
Pelican Books, 1937), Foreword, p. vii. The relation of
philosophy to science is curiously misunderstood by some
scientists. It is true that "few in this age would willingly
base their lives on a philosophy which to the man of
science is demonstrably false." But it does not follow
that "science thus takes the place of the foundation on
which the structure of our lives must be built if we wish
that structure to be stable." Arthur H. Compton, *The Religion of a Scientist* (New York, The Jewish Theological
Seminary of America, 1938), p. 5. First of all, science
itself is not stable. Secondly, from the fact that no set of
propositions can be held as true if it contradicts another
set of propositions that are demonstrably true, it does not
follow that this second set of propositions must provide
the foundation whereupon to establish our lives. It is
quite possible, for instance, that the philosophical propositions whereupon we must establish our lives are quite
independent of all conceivable sets of scientific propositions.

is not mysterious, what is? In 1930, in his Rede Lecture delivered before the University of Cambridge, Sir James Jeans decided to deal with philosophical problems in the light of contemporary science. The upshot was his most popular book: *The Mysterious Universe*. Now, if the universe of science is mysterious, what is not? We do not need science to tell us that the universe is indeed mysterious. Men have known that since the very beginning of the human race. The true and proper function of science is, on the contrary, to make as much of the universe as possible grow less and less mysterious to us. Science does it, and she does it magnificently. Any sixteen-year-old boy, in any one of our schools, knows more today about the physical structure of the world than Thomas Aquinas, Aristotle, or Plato ever did. He can give rational explanations of phenomena which once appeared to the greatest minds as puzzling mysteries. The universe of science *qua* science exactly consists of that part of the total universe from which, owing to human reason, mysteries have been removed.

How is it, then, that a scientist can feel well founded in calling this universe a "mysterious universe"? Is it because the very progress of science brings him face to face with phe-

nomena that are more and more difficult to ob-
serve and whose laws are more and more difficult to formulate? But the unknown is not
necessarily a mystery; and science naturally
proceeds upon the assumption that it is not,
because it is at least knowable, even though we
do not yet know it. The true reason why this
universe appears to some scientists as mysterious is that, mistaking existential, that is, metaphysical, questions for scientific ones, they ask
science to answer them. Naturally, they get
no answers. Then they are puzzled, and they
say that the universe is mysterious.

The scientific cosmogony of Sir James
Jeans himself exhibits an instructive collec-
tion of such perplexities. His starting point is
the actual existence of innumerable stars
"wandering about space" at such enormous
distances from one another "that it is an event
of almost unimaginable rarity for a star to
come anywhere near to another star." Yet, we
must "believe" that "some two thousand mil-
lion years ago, this rare event took place, and
that a second star, wandering blindly through
space," happened to come so near the sun that
it raised a huge tidal wave on its surface. This
mountainous wave finally exploded, and its
fragments, still "circulating around their parent sun . . . are the planets, great and small,

of which our earth is one." These ejected fragments of the sun gradually cooled; "in course
of time, we know not how, when, or why, one
of these cooling fragments gave birth to life."
Hence, the emergence of a stream of life which
has culminated in man. In a universe where
empty space is deadly cold and most of the
matter deadly hot, the emergence of life was
highly improbable. Nevertheless, "into such a
universe we have stumbled, if not exactly by
mistake, at least as the result of what may
properly be described as an accident." Such
is, Sir James Jeans concludes, "the surprising
manner in which, so far as science can at present inform us, we came into being."[8]

That all this is very mysterious everybody
will agree, but the question then arises: Is this
science? Even if we take them, as their author
evidently does, for so many "provisional hypotheses," can we consider such hypotheses as
being, in any sense of the word, scientific? Is it
scientific to explain the existence of man by a
series of accidents, each of which is more improbable than the other one? The truth of the
case simply is that on the problem of the existence of man modern astronomy has strictly
nothing to say. And the same conclusion holds
good if, to modern astronomy, we add modern

8. Sir James Jeans, *op. cit.*, chap. i, pp. 11–22.

physics. When, after describing the physical world of Einstein, Heisenberg, Dirac, Lemaître, and Louis de Broglie, he at last takes a dive into what, this time at least, he knows to be "the deep waters" of metaphysics, what conclusion does Sir James Jeans ultimately reach? That although many scientists prefer the notion of a "cyclic universe, the more orthodox scientific view" is that this universe owes its present form to a "creation" and that "its creation must have been an act of thought."[9] Granted. But what have these answers to do with Einstein, Heisenberg, and the justly famous galaxy of modern physicists? The two doctrines of a "cyclical universe" and of a supreme Thought were formulated by pre-Socratic philosophers who knew nothing of what Einstein would say twenty-six centuries after them. "Modern scientific theory," Jeans adds, "compels us to think of the creator as working outside time and space, which are part of his creation, just as the artist is outside his canvas."[10] Why should modern theory compel us to say what has already been said, not only by Saint Augustine, whom our scientist quotes, but by any and every one of countless Christian theologians who knew no

9. *Ibid.*, chap. v, p. 182.
10. *Ibid.*, chap. v, p. 183.

other world than that of Ptolemy? Clearly
enough, the philosophical answer of Sir
James Jeans to the problem of the world
order has absolutely nothing to do with modern science. And no wonder, since it has absolutely nothing to do with any scientific knowledge at all.

If we consider it more closely, the initial
question asked by Jeans had taken him at
once not only into deep waters but, scientifically speaking, out of soundings. To ask the
question why, out of an infinity of possible
combinations of physicochemical elements,
there has arisen the living and thinking being
we call man is to seek the cause why such a
complex of physical energies as man actually
is, or exists. In other words, it is to inquire
into the possible causes for the *existence* of
living and thinking organisms upon earth.
The hypothesis that living substances may to-
morrow be produced by biochemists in their
laboratories is irrelevant to the question. If a
chemist ever succeeds in turning out living
cells, or some elementary sorts of organisms,
nothing will be easier for him than to say why
such organisms exist. His answer will be: I
made them. Our own question is not at all:
Are living and thinking beings made up of
nothing else than physical elements? It rather

is: Supposing they ultimately consist of nothing else, how can we account for the *existence*
of the very order of molecules which produces
what we call life, and thought?

Scientifically speaking, such problems do
not make sense. If there were no living and
thinking beings, there would be no science.
Hence there would be no questions. Even the
scientific universe of inorganic matter is a
structural universe; as to the world of organic
matter, it everywhere exhibits coördination,
adaptation, functions. When asked why there
are such organized beings, scientists answer:
Chance. Now anybody may fluke a brilliant
stroke at billiards; but when a billiard player
makes a run of a hundred, to say that he
fluked it is to offer a rather weak explanation.
Some scientists know this so well that they
substitute for the notion of chance the notion
of mechanical laws, which is its very reverse.
But when they come to explaining how these
mechanical laws have given rise to living organized beings, they are driven back to chance
as to the last reason it is possible to quote.
"The powers operating in the cosmos," Julian
Huxley says, "are, though unitary, yet subdivisible; and, though subdivisible, yet related. There are the vast powers of inorganic
nature, neutral or hostile to man. Yet they

gave birth to evolving life, whose development, though blind and fortuitous, has tended
in the same general direction as our own conscious desires and ideals, and so gives us an
external sanction for our directional activi-
ties. This again gave birth to human mind,
which, in the race, is changing the course of
evolution by acceleration,"[11] and so on, ad infinitum. In other words, the only scientific
reasons why our billiard player makes a run
of a hundred are that he cannot play billiards
and that all the chances are against it.

If scientists, speaking as scientists, have no
intelligible answer to this problem, why are
some of them so keen on talking nonsense
about it? The reason is simple, and this time
we can be sure that chance has nothing to do
with their obstinacy. They prefer to say anything rather than to ascribe existence to God
on the ground that a purpose exists in the universe. Now there is some justification for
their attitude. Just as science can play havoc
with metaphysics, metaphysics can play havoc
with science. Coming before science in the
past, it has often done so to the point of pre-

11. Julian Huxley, "Rationalism and the Idea of God,"
in *Essays of a Biologist,* chap. vi (London, Pelican Books,
1939), p. 176. This "scientific" cosmogony strangely resembles the *Theogony* of Hesiod, where everything is successively begotten from original Chaos.

venting its rise and of blocking its development. For centuries final causes have been mistaken for scientific explanations by so many generations of philosophers that today many scientists still consider the fear of final causes as the beginning of scientific wisdom. Science is thus making metaphysics suffer for its centuries-long meddling in matters of physics and biology.

In both cases, however, the real victim of this epistemological strife is one and the same: the human mind. Nobody denies that living organisms appear as though they had been designed, or intended, to fulfill the various functions related to life. Everybody agrees that this appearance may be but an illusion. We would be bound to hold it for an illusion if science could account for the rise of life by its usual explanations of mechanical type, where nothing more is involved than the relations of observable phenomena according to the geometrical properties of space and the physical laws of motion. What is most remarkable, on the contrary, is that many scientists obstinately maintain the illusory character of this appearance though they freely acknowledge their failure to imagine any scientific explanation for the organic constitution of living beings. As soon as modern physics had reached the structural problems raised by molecular physics, it found itself confronted with such difficulties. Yet scientists much preferred to introduce into physics the nonmechanical notions of discontinuity and indeterminacy rather than resort to anything like design. On a much larger scale, we have seen Julian Huxley boldly account for the existence of organized bodies by those very properties of matter which, according to himself, make it infinitely improbable that such bodies should ever exist. Why should those eminently rational beings, the scientists, deliberately prefer to the simple notions of design, or purposiveness, in nature, the arbitrary notions of blind force, chance, emergence, sudden variation, and similar ones? Simply because they much prefer a complete absence of intelligibility to the presence of a nonscientific intelligibility.

We seem to be here reaching at last the very core of this epistemological problem. Unintelligible as they are, these arbitrary notions are at least homogeneous with a chain of mechanical interpretations. Posited at the beginning of such a chain, or inserted in it where they are needed, they provide the scientist with the very existences which he needs in order to have something to know.

Their very irrationality is expressive of the invincible resistance opposed by existence to any type of scientific explanation.[12] By accepting design, or purposiveness, as a possible principle of explanation, a scientist would introduce into his system of laws a ring wholly heterogeneous with the rest of the chain. He would intertwine the metaphysical causes for the existence of organisms with the physical causes which he must assign to both their structure and their functioning. Still worse, he might feel tempted to mistake the existential causes of living organisms for their efficient and physical causes, thus coming back to the good old times when fishes had fins because they had been made to swim. Now it may well be true that fishes have been made to swim, but when we know it we know just as much about fishes as we know about airplanes when we know that they are made to fly. If they had not been made to fly, there would be no airplanes, since to be flying-machines is their very definition; but it takes us at least two

12. The marked antipathy of modern science toward the notion of efficient cause is intimately related to the nonexistential character of scientific explanations. It is of the essence of an efficient cause that it makes something be, or exist. Since the relation of effect to cause is an existential and a nonanalytical one, it appears to the scientific mind as a sort of scandal which must be eliminated.

sciences, aerodynamics and mechanics, in
order to know how they do fly. A final cause
has posited an existence whose science alone
can posit the laws.

This heterogeneity of these two orders was
strikingly expressed by Francis Bacon, when
he said, speaking of final causes, that "in
physics, they are impertinent, and as remoras
to the ship, that hinder the sciences from hold-
ing their course of improvement."[13] Their
scientific sterility is particularly complete in
a world like that of modern science, where essences have been reduced to mere phenomena,
themselves reduced to the order of that which
can be observed. Modern scientists live, or
they pretend to live, in a world of mere ap-
pearances, where that which appears is the
appearance of nothing. Yet the fact that final
causes are scientifically sterile does not entail
their disqualification as metaphysical causes,
and to reject metaphysical answers to a problem just because they are not scientific is deliberately to maim the knowing power of the

13. Francis Bacon, *The Dignity and Advancement of
Learning*, Bk. III, chap. iv, ed. J. E. Creighton (New
York, The Colonial Press, 1900), p. 97. Cf. p. 98: "These
final causes, however, are not false, or unworthy of inquiry in metaphysics, but their excursion into the limits
of physical causes has made a great devastation in that
province."

human mind. If the only intelligible way to explain the existence of organized bodies is to admit that there is design, purposiveness, at their origin, then let us admit it, if not as scientists, at least as metaphysicians. And since the notions of design and of purpose are for us inseparable from the notion of thought, to posit the existence of a thought as cause of the purposiveness of organized bodies is also to posit an end of all ends, or an ultimate end, that is, God.

It goes without saying that this is the very consequence which the adversaries of final causes intend to deny. "Purpose," Julian Huxley says, "is a psychological term; and to ascribe purpose to a process merely because its results are somewhat similar to those of a true purposeful process is completely unjustified, and a mere projection of our own ideas into the economy of nature."[14] This is most certainly what we do, but why should we not do so? We do not need to *project* our own ideas into the economy of nature; they belong there in their own right. Our own ideas are in the economy of nature because we ourselves are in it. Any and every one of the things which a man does intelligently is done with a purpose and to a certain end which is the final

14. Julian Huxley, *op. cit.*, chap. vi, p. 173.

cause why he does it. Whatever a worker, an engineer, an industrialist, a writer, or an artist makes is but the actualization, by intelligently selected means, of a certain end. There is no known example of a self-made machine spontaneously arising in virtue of the mechanical laws of matter. Through man, who is part and parcel of nature, purposiveness most certainly is part and parcel of nature. In what sense then is it arbitrary, knowing from within that where there is organization there always is a purpose, to conclude that there is a purpose wherever there is organization? I fully understand a scientist who turns down such an inference as wholly nonscientific. I also understand a scientist who tells me that, as a scientist, he has no business to draw any inference as to the possible cause why organized bodies actually exist. But I wholly fail to see in what sense my inference, if I choose to draw it, is "a common fallacy."

Why should there be a fallacy in inferring that there is purpose in the universe on the ground of biological progress? Because, Julian Huxley answers, this "can be shown to be as natural and inevitable a product of the struggle for existence as is adaptation, and to be no more mysterious than, for instance, the increase in effectiveness both of armour-piercing projectile and armour-plate during the last century."[15] Does Julian Huxley suggest that steel plates have spontaneously grown thicker as shells were growing heavier during the last century? In other words, does he maintain that purposiveness is as wholly absent from human industry as it is from the rest of the world? Or does he perhaps maintain that the rest of the world is as full of purposiveness as human industry obviously is? In the name of science he maintains both, namely, that adaptations in organisms are no more mysterious where there is no purposiveness to account for them, than is adaptation in human industry where purposiveness everywhere accounts for it. That adaptations due to a purpose*less* struggle for life are no more mysterious than adaptations due to a purpose*ful* struggle—whether this proposition is "a common fallacy," I do not know, but it certainly seems to be a fallacy. It is the fallacy of a scientist who, because he does not know how to ask metaphysical problems, obstinately refuses their correct metaphysical answers. In the *Inferno* of the world of knowledge, there is a special punishment for this sort of sin; it is the relapse into mythology. Better known as a distinguished zoologist, Julian Huxley

15. *Ibid.*, p. 172.

must also be credited with having added the god Struggle to the already large family of the Olympians.[16]

A world which has lost the Christian God cannot but resemble a world which had not yet found him. Just like the world of Thales and of Plato, our own modern world is "full of gods." There are blind Evolution, clear-sighted Orthogenesis, benevolent Progress, and others which it is more advisable not to mention by name. Why unnecessarily hurt the feelings of men who, today, render them a cult? It is however important for us to realize that mankind is doomed to live more and more under the spell of a new scientific, social, and political mythology, unless we resolutely exorcise these befuddled notions whose influence on modern life is becoming appalling. Millions of men are starving and bleeding to death because two or three of these pseudo-scientific or pseudosocial deified abstractions are now at war. For when gods fight among themselves, men have to die. Could we not make an effort to realize that evolution is to be largely what we will make it to be? That

16. On the philosophical difficulties entailed by this notion of evolution, see W. R. Thompson, *Science and Common Sense*, pp. 216–232.

Progress is not an automatically self-achiev-
ing law but something to be patiently achieved
by the will of men? That Equality is not an
actually given fact but an ideal to be progressively approached by means of justice?
That Democracy is not the leading goddess of
some societies but a magnificent promise to be
fulfilled by all through their obstinate will for
friendship, if they are strong enough to make
it last for generations after generations?

I think we could, but a good deal of clear
thinking should come first, and this is where,
in spite of its proverbial helplessness, philosophy might be of some help. The trouble
with so many of our contemporaries is not
that they are agnostics but rather that they
are misguided theologians. Real agnostics are
exceedingly rare, and they harm nobody but
themselves. Just as they have no God, these
have no gods. Much more common, unfortu-
nately, are those pseudo-agnostics who, because they combine scientific knowledge and
social generosity with a complete lack of
philosophical culture, substitute dangerous
mythologies for the natural theology which
they do not even understand.

The problem of final causes is perhaps the
problem most commonly discussed by these

modern agnostics. As such, it particularly recommended itself to cur attention. It is nevertheless only one among the many aspects of the highest of all metaphysical problems, that of Being. Beyond the question: Why are there organized beings? lies this deeper one, which I am asking in Leibniz's own terms: Why is there something rather than nothing? Here again, I fully understand a scientist who refuses to ask it. He is welcome to tell me that the question does not make sense. Scientifically speaking, it does not.[17] Metaphysi-

17. The hostility exhibited by a wholly mathematized science toward the irreducible act of existence is what lies behind its opposition, so well marked by H. Bergson, to duration itself. Malebranche considered the existence of matter as indemonstrable; hence his conclusion that the annihilation of the material world by God would in no way affect our scientific knowledge of it. Sir Arthur Eddington would certainly not subscribe to Malebranche's metaphysics; but his own approach to the problem of existence is an epistemological one, namely, this particular body of knowledge which we call modern physics; hence the analogous consequence that, from such a point of view, "the question of attributing a mysterious property called *existence* to the physical universe never arises." *The Philosophy of Physical Science* (Cambridge, University Press, 1939), chap. x, pp. 156–157. As a substitute for the "metaphysical concept of *real existence*," Sir Arthur offers a "structural concept of existence," which he defines in pp. 162–166. In point of fact, there is a metaphysical concept of *being,* which is not "hazy" (p. 162), but analogical; as to actual existence, it is not an object of concept, but of judgment. To substitute "struc-

cally speaking, however, it does. Science can
account for many things in the world; it may
some day account for all that which the world
of phenomena actually is. But why anything
at all is, or exists, science knows not, precisely because it cannot even ask the question.

To this supreme question, the only conceivable answer is that each and every particular existential energy, each and every particular existing thing, depends for its existence upon a pure Act of existence.[18] In order

tural existence" for "real existence" is to be headed for
the conclusion that "independent existence" is, for a
given element, "its existence as a contributor to the structure," whereas its nonexistence is "a hole occurring in, or
added to, the structure" (p. 165). In other words, the *independent* existence, or nonexistence, of an element is
strictly dependent upon its whole. To exist is "to be a-
contributor-to"; to cease to exist is to cease "to be
a-contributor-to." Yet, in order to be a contributor to
some whole, a thing has first to be; and to define the
death of a man by the hole it creates in his family is to
take a rather detached view of what appears to the dying
man himself as an intensely individuated event.

18. Sir Arthur Eddington complains that philosophers
do nothing to make clear to "laymen" what the word "existence" means. *The Philosophy of Physical Science,* chap.
x, pp. 154–157. As an example of its ambiguity, Sir
Arthur quotes the judgment: There is an overdraft at the
bank. Is an "overdraft at a bank" something that exists?
The answer is: Yes, and no. The verbal form "is" has two
distinct meanings, according as it designates: (1) the
actual existence of a thing; (2) the composition of a
predicate with a subject in a judgment. What exists at

to be the ultimate answer to all existential problems, this supreme cause has to be absolute existence.[19] Being absolute, such a cause is self-sufficient; if it creates, its creative act must be free. Since it creates not only being but order, it must be something which at least eminently contains the only principle of order known to us in experience, namely, thought. Now an absolute, self-subsisting, and knowing cause is not an It but a He. In short, the first

the bank, in sense number one, is a draft; but it is true, in sense number two, that "this draft is an overdraft." To say that "a draft is an overdraft," is by no means to say that an "overdraft" actually is, or exists.

19. Some scientists, who still realize the value of the argument on the basis of design, would say that they do not feel "the need of a Creator to start the Universe." A. H. Compton, *The Religion of a Scientist,* p. 11. In other words, they do not realize that these two problems are identically the same. Design appears to them as a fact whose *existence* calls for an explanation. Why then should not the protons, electrons, neutrons, and photons be considered as facts whose *existence* also calls for some explanation? In what sense is the existence of these elements less mysterious than that of their composite? What prevents many scientists from going as far as to ask this second question is that, this time, they cannot fail to perceive the nonscientific character of the problem. Yet the nature of the two problems is the same. If the cause for the *existence* of organisms lies outside the nature of their physicochemical elements, it transcends the physical order; hence it is transphysical, that is, metaphysical, in its own right. In other words, if there is nothing in the elements to account for design, the presence of design in a chaos of elements entails just as necessarily a *creation* as the very existence of the elements.

cause is the One in whom the cause of both
nature and history coincide, a philosophical
God who can also be the God of a religion.[20]

To go one step further would be to match
the mistake of some agnostics with a similar
one. The failure of too many metaphysicians
to distinguish between philosophy and religion has proved no less harmful to natural
theology than have the encroachments of
pseudometaphysical science. Metaphysics pos-

20. Dr. A. H. Compton is an interesting instance of
those many scientists who do not seem to be aware of
crossing any border lines when they pass from science to
philosophy and from philosophy to religion. To them the
"hypothesis God" is just one more of those "working
hypotheses" which a scientist provisorily accepts as true
in spite of the fact that none of them can be proved.
Hence the consequence that "faith in God may be a
thoroughly scientific attitude, even though we may be
unable to establish the correctness of our belief." *The Religion of a Scientist,* p. 13. This is a regrettable confusion
of language. It is true the principle of the conservation
of energy and the notion of evolution are hypotheses; but
they are *scientific* hypotheses because, according as we
accept or reject them, our scientific interpretation of observable facts is bound to become different. The existence
or nonexistence of God, on the contrary, is a proposition
whose negation or affirmation determines no change whatever in the structure of our scientific explanation of the
world and is wholly independent of the contents of
science as such. Supposing, for instance, there be design
in the world, the existence of God cannot be posited as a
scientific explanation for the presence of design in the
world; it is a *metaphysical* one; consequently, God has not
to be posited as a *scientific probability* but as a *metaphysical necessity.*

its God as a pure Act of existence, but it
does not provide us with any concept of His
essence. We know that He is; we do not com-
prehend Him. Simple-minded metaphysicians
have unwillingly led agnostics to believe that
the God of natural theology was the "watchmaker" of Voltaire, or the "carpenter" of
cheap apologetics. First of all, no watch has
ever been made by any watchmaker; "watch-
makers" as such simply do not exist; watches
are made by men who know how to make
watches. Similarly, to posit God as the supreme cause of that which is, is to know that
He is He who can create, because He is "He
who is"; but this tells us still less concerning
what absolute existence can be than any piece
of carpentry tells us about the man who made
it. Being men, we can affirm God only on anthropomorphic grounds, but this does not
oblige us to posit Him as an anthropomorphic
God. As Saint Thomas Aquinas says:

The verb *to be* is used in two different ways:
in a first one, it signifies the act of existing
(*actu essendi*); in the second one it signifies the
composition of those propositions which the
soul invents by joining a predicate with a subject. Taking *to be* in the first way, we cannot
know the "to be" of God (*esse Dei*), no more
than we know His essence. We know it in the

second way only. For, indeed, we know that the
proposition we are forming about God, when we
say: God is, is a true proposition, and we know
this from His effects.[21]

If such be the God of natural theology,
true metaphysics does not culminate in a concept, be it that of Thought, of Good, of One,
or of Substance. It does not even culminate in
an essence, be it that of Being itself. Its last
word is not *ens*, but *esse;* not *being*, but *is*.
The ultimate effort of true metaphysics is to
posit an Act by an act, that is, to posit by an
act of judging the supreme Act of existing
whose very essence, because it is to be, passes
human understanding. Where a man's metaphysics comes to an end, his religion begins.
But the only path which can lead him to the
point where the true religion begins must of
necessity lead him beyond the contemplation
of essences, up to the very mystery of existence. This path is not very hard to find, but
few are those who dare to follow it to the end.
Seduced as they are by the intelligible beauty
of science, many men lose all taste for metaphysics and religion. A few others, absorbed
in the contemplation of some supreme cause,
become aware that metaphysics and religion

21. Saint Thomas Aquinas, *Summa theologica,* Pars I,
qu. 3, art. 4, ad 2ᵐ.

should ultimately meet, but they cannot tell
how or where; hence they separate religion
from philosophy, or else they renounce religion for philosophy, if they do not, like Pascal, renounce philosophy for religion. Why
should not we keep truth, and keep it whole?
It can be done. But only those can do it who
realize that He Who is the God of the philosophers is HE WHO IS, the God of Abraham,
of Isaac, and of Jacob.

INDEX

Note. References other than those to proper names are incomplete. They are included as a guide to important sections not indicated by proper name references.

Due